Islam, Terrorism
and
Your Future

Islam, Terrorism and Your Future

by
Isaac ben Abraham

CEDAR HILL PRESS

ISBN 0-9702138-1-6

First Edition
Printed in the United States of America
1 2 3 4 5 6 7 — 06 05 04 03 02 01

CONTENTS

Preface
vii

Introduction:
A Search for Meaning
ix

Chapter 1:
Who Are We Fighting?
1

Chapter 2:
The Basics of Islam: The Prophet and the Koran
7

Chapter 3:
Are Jehovah and Allah the Same God?
24

Chapter 4:
Different Prescriptions for Living
39

Chapter 5:
Jihad
51

Chapter 6:
The Goal of a World Empire
63

Chapter 7:
All Roads Lead to Israel
74

Chapter 8:
Oil—The Fuel that Funds
87

Chapter 9:
The Spread of Islamic Wildfire
95

Chapter 10:
Our Response as Americans and as Christians
105

PREFACE

In writing this book, I have deliberately chosen not to be scholarly or technical because I want to spare readers the need to refer constantly to a lexicon or dictionary. I have used Westernized spellings of Arab names, as those names are commonly found in popular American periodicals.

I am writing this book from a viewpoint that many Westerners do not have. I know the Middle East. I have first-hand experience with Islamic practices and thought processes.

My love for freedom and democracy that are embodied in America compels me to write this book.

I have tried to distinguish between Islam as a religious system and Muslims as people. I love the people who embrace Islam—many of them are friends and acquaintances. While I risk being criticized for my sociological, economical, and political assessments, my ardent desire is that no one misunderstand my genuine love and deep appreciation for Muslim people.

From my perspective as a Christian, I see all other religious systems as less than whole. The God who revealed Himself in the person of Jesus Christ tells us that without the one Savior, no one can be accepted by the Father.

I do not look down on Muslims. On the contrary, I yearn for them to know the fullness of life that comes only through Jesus Christ.

INTRODUCTION

A Search for Meaning

Americans felt blind-sided on September 11, 2001. Never before had so many private citizens been killed by foreign nationals. Most who saw the towers of the World Trade Center collapse, the smoldering gaping hole in the Pentagon, and heard the story of the final minutes of a doomed flight that ended in a Pennsylvania field, felt a visceral, emotional pain and sorrow. Our soul as a nation had been wounded.

Many also felt themselves adrift in a sea of confusion. Terrorism always leaves a wake of confusion. Why did this happen? Why us? Why do these people hate us so? What next? When will the next attack come? What will it be and who will be hit?

Slowly, as the dust settled and the days passed, many Americans began to face the fact that they had been *targeted for their beliefs and values.*

Prior to September 11, 2001, many in the United States seemed to regard Islamic-rooted terrorism as being against our "political system." Targets in recent years had been two U.S. Embassies in distant Africa, a U.S. Navy ship (the USS Cole), and U.S. Marines barracks—one in Saudi Arabia, another even longer ago in Lebanon. Targets against civilians were seen as anomalies, including the initial bombing at the base of the World Trade Center in February of

1993. The prevailing opinion seemed to be, "Muslim extremists obviously don't like our government—perhaps not even our institutions—but surely they like *us* as a people."

On September 11, 2001, Islamic-rooted terrorism attacked United States citizens—ordinary, hard-working, brilliant individuals who were going about their normal everyday work. Even the attack on the Pentagon can be perceived as an attack on the people who worked there since no military hardware or installations were involved.

Governments are a reflection of policies, institutions, treaties, political agreements, and political alliances. "Average citizens," on the other hand, are the embodiment of culture and religion. It became clear to many—perhaps not the first day but certainly in the months that followed—that America was being targeted for its most basic beliefs.

September 11, 2001 is a date that will ring in the lives of all who experienced it as a day of horror, infamy, assault, sorrow, and in many respects, a day of "eye-opening truth."

New questions require answers: What is it the terrorists hate? What is it they want? What are their ultimate goals? And *why* do they do what they do?

This book aims to answer those questions—certainly not in full detail in a book of this length, but in broad summary. This book presents historical facts, theological insights, and quotes that have been published or aired by leading media providers. An attempt has been made to be as factual and objective as possible, but the perspective is unashamedly pro-American and Christian. We are the ones who have been attacked, and it is from *our* perspective as Americans and Christians that we must seek understanding and an appropriate response. The search for answers must begin with an assessment of Islam.

Chapter One

WHO ARE WE FIGHTING?

This is not a war against Islam.
—President George W. Bush

O ne of the most admirable aspects of our national response to the September 11, 2001 attack on the United States has been a general reluctance to declare ourselves to be in a religious war. Government officials and media commentators have repeatedly stressed that point. President Bush went to the Islamic Center in Washington to reinforce his statement, and public prayer meetings across the United States and throughout the Western world have included Muslim leaders alongside Christians, Jews, and Buddhists.

Americans need to be acutely aware, however, that Islam has declared war on Christianity, and in particular, on the United States of America as the leading nation of the West and of Christendom. Religion *is* at the heart of the conflict.

We may not want to be at war with Islam, but Islam chooses to be at war with us. In this case, reality is in the perception of the perpetrator.

Osama bin Laden's statements in the aftermath of the attack, as well as in months and years preceding it, are saturated with religious arguments and theological language. He said in 1998:

> The call to wage war against America was made because
> America has spearheaded the crusade against the Islamic

nation, sending tens of thousands of its troops to the land of the two holy mosques over and above its meddling in its affairs and its politics and its support of the oppressive, corrupt, and tyrannical regime that is in control." [Quoted in Andrew Sullivan, "This *Is* a Religious War" *New York Times Magazine* October 10, 2001]

Osama bin Laden's use of the word "crusade" is an explicitly religious term—and the Islamic nation is not just one political nation, but rather, Islam reflected in many nations and many ethnicities. He clearly saw the war as being against "unbelief and unbelievers" and regarded the conflict as a noble cause:

"We have been entrusted with good cause to follow in the footsteps of the messenger [Muhammad] and to communicate his message to all nations." (Andrew Sullivan, "This *Is* a Religious War" *New York Times Magazine* October 10, 2001)

Bin Laden has also stated that his particular brand of terrorism was "of the commendable kind, for it is directed at the tyrants and the aggressors and enemies of Allah." (*ibid*)

The Taliban regime in Afghanistan was openly and fanatically religious. While some Muslim leaders criticized the terrorists and have distanced themselves from militant Islamic factions, many others in the Middle East and elsewhere have not denounced the acts of September 11. They have been almost conspicuous in their silence.

Other Voices from the Islamic World

There have also been those who have said that this is not a war of Islam versus Christianity and Judaism, but rather, a war of "fundamentalism" against faiths of all kinds that are at peace with freedom and modernity. This certainly sounds like the politically correct approach to take—something of a "high road"'—but again, facts don't bear out such an ideal.

It is a fact that true Christian fundementalism is rooted in the model of Christ with His teaching and example of turning the other cheek.

By contrast, what we have seen in the aftermath of September 11, 2001, are *very few* voices from the Islamic world that denounce

Islamic fundamentalism. A few statements were made initially, within hours and days of the attack, but very few statements have been made subsequently, and certainly not after the launching of military action in Afghanistan. The Islamic world has been almost universally void of applause for the collapse of the Taliban.

Queen Rania of Jordan appeared on the Oprah Winfrey program October 9, 2001. Oprah asked her, "When this first happened on September 11, I think it came as a shock to so many of us that other people in the world hated us so much. Can you help explain that to us?"

The thirty-one-year-old Queen responded this way:

> I think it's very important that you realize that for the majority of Muslims, they do not hate Americans. They do not hate the American way of life. In fact, many countries look at the American model as one that needs to be replicated, one that they aspire to achieve.
>
> We are talking about a minority of people who feel that they have been unjustly treated by the United States. Some of them feel that U.S. foreign policy might have been partial and not completely fair to all parties involved, and they wanted their voice to be heard. Unfortunately, the means that they have used are ones that are condemned all over the Arab world.

Sadly, she is in error. There has been no widespread indication that the majority of Muslims condemn terrorism. Those who have spoken against terrorism have not spoken loudly and very importantly, have not spoken to *their own people*.

We should not be entirely surprised at this.

Historically, radical Islamic actions have rarely been denounced.

What we have heard from Muslims are questions as to whether Osama bin Laden and Al Qaeda were behind the September 11 attack. Literally millions of Muslims around the world flat-out refused to believe that Muslims were involved in the September 11 attack. They repeatedly made statements such as this one by a young teenager in an Islamic school just outside Washington, D.C.: "The terrorists who hit the World Trade Center and the Pentagon may have claimed to be Muslims, but since Islam forbids the killing of innocents, those killers are by definition not

3

Muslim." Some contend the terrorists weren't Muslim prior to the attack, others that they lost their status and definition as Muslim by engaging in the attack.

Many others did not question the identity of the terrorists—they openly accepted the fact that they were Muslims and they cheered their bravery, calling them "martyrs" for Islam:

- In Egypt, university students burned U.S. and Israeli flags and chanted, "Arrogant George Bush, tomorrow you will reap the fruits of your war!"
- In Indonesia, hundreds of Islamic activists clashed with police outside the U.S. Embassy in Jakarta.
- In Sudan, protesters tried to storm the U.S. Embassy in Khartoum.
- In the Philippines, about five thousand protesters chanted "Death to America" and "Long live Osama bin Laden" as they burned American flags and a picture of President Bush in a Muslim-dominated region.
- Muslim leaders in Malawi warned Americans they were not safe.
- In Malaysia, the Pan-Malaysia Islamic Party called upon the United Nations to declare the United States a terrorist state.
- In the Gaza strip, two Palestinians were killed and 76 people were injured in protests against the United States.

As the United States geared up to respond to Al Qaeda terrorist camps and the Taliban regime that harbored Al Qaeda in Afghanistan, the Secretary-General of the Arab League, Amr Moussa, said in Qatar, "Any military strike to any Arab country will lead to serious consequences and will be considered an aggression against Arab states."

Echoes of the Ayatollah Khomeini

The response from the Arab world as a whole, and especially from certain militant factions of Islam, is reminiscent of the rhetoric heard more than two decades ago in Iran.

In 1979, as the Ayatollah Khomeini responded to the taking of fifty-two Americans hostage in Tehran, he said, "This is not a struggle between the United States and Iran. It is a struggle between Islam and the infidels." He further declared, "The governments of the world should know that Islam cannot be defeated. Islam will be victorious in all the countries of the world, and Islam and all the teachings of the Koran will prevail all over the world."

Khomeini was not speaking as a lone voice. He was expressing what lies at the heart of all fervent believers in Islam.

The words of Khomeini made little sense to Westerners. To Muslims they made perfect sense. Some Islamic moderates wished he had not been so fanatically blunt. But Islamic moderates are becoming a minority on the world scene. It is the extremist Muslims who grab the headlines. And as never before, they are affirming their spiritual identity and flexing their political and economic muscles to promote the Islamic way of life.

We should also note at the outset that the spread of Islam today is greater than at any other time in history. Islam has between one billion and 1.5 billion adherents today—one out of five people in the world are Muslims. Islam reigns as the dominant religion in forty-five "Muslim nations."

With the spread of Islam as a whole has come the spread of *militant* Islam (which is the true and original Islam) and the opinions of Khomeini and others like him.

In dealing with Islamic terrorists we need to recognize several historical and theological facts:

- **All of the terrorists being targeted in the present War on Terrorism are Muslims.** Historically, encounters between Islam and Christianity have often resulted in war.

- **Islam and Christianity do not worship the SAME God.** Islam, Judaism, and Christianity are all monotheistic—they each advocate the reality of one god. The only trait Allah and Jehovah hold in common, however, is this: God is Creator of all.

- **Islam and Christianity differ greatly in beliefs about Jesus.** Muslims regard Christians as blasphemers for proclaiming that Jesus Christ is the Son of God. They regard Muhammad as the only true prophet. Christians, in turn, regard Jesus as divine and the savior of all mankind; they regard Muhammad as a misguided come-lately religious man.

- **Islam and Christianity have historically used very different means to further their cause.** Islam advances on the groundswell of *power*. It seeks submission, humiliation, and conquest of all who do not believe in Islam. Christianity, in sharp contrast, advances on the groundswell of personal conversion. It seeks the renewal of the human heart, which in turn, will result in obedience to God's commands.

Islam is a religion steeped in revenge and retaliation. Christianity is a religion steeped in spiritual renewal, based on a personal relationship with God through Christ.

We Must Open Our Eyes

The time for a naïve look at the world is over. We must open our eyes to see that the real cause of terrorism is hate. Hate is a belief. We must ask repeatedly, "Who and what is being hated?" What we hate is what we attack. What we hate is what we seek to destroy or subjugate.

Tens of millions of Muslims *hate* all that Christians believe, create, administrate, and advocate. To destroy Christianity, Muslims seek the lives of Christians.

We also must recognize that even if the radical fringe in the Muslim movement is silenced or defeated militarily, it will not "diminish." New expressions will emerge—some, perhaps, more subtle, and others, perhaps even more violent than what has been experienced in the past. The war against terrorism is ultimately a war for the human heart.

We are not only engaged in a battle to dismantle funding sources, terrorist training camps, lines of communication, and organizations. Ultimately, we are in an ideological battle that is very real, very intense, and of eternal significance.

We must open our eyes to our real enemy—the spirit of Islam—and then seek to learn as much as possible about it.

Chapter Two

THE BASICS OF ISLAM: THE PROPHET AND THE KORAN

U ntil the seventh century, relatively little is known about the people and culture of Arabia, the peninsula now occupied by Saudi Arabia, Oman, United Arab Emirates, Qatar, Bahrain, and Yemen. A stream of caravan traders routinely crossed the peninsula, making it the commercial land-link between the Mediterranean and Far East. Three major towns sprung up in northern Arabia to service this trade route, the most prosperous and important of these being Mecca, which was a bustling city by 600 A.D.

The people who lived on this peninsula had a faith rooted deeply in idolatry. For centuries, the Arabians had withstood every attempt by Christians from Syria and Egypt to convert them. Each of the nomadic Bedouin tribes living in the vast desert worshiped a variety of its own deities and nature spirits, although a few gods were revered in common. The Kaaba was the shrine to these commonly acknowledged deities. *Kaaba* literally means "cube" or "the heal of the foot." It is a large cubical structure in a massive courtyard area in Mecca.

Muhammad is credited with expelling the former deities from the Kaaba and making the Kaaba the central shrine of the new religion of Islam. It remains the focal point of Islamic worship today. Nobody but Muslims are allowed there. Those who make a pilgrimage to Mecca walk around the Kaaba seven times, kissing and touching the Black Stone at its center. Muslims know the site as "the house of Allah."

Legend attributes the building of the Kaaba to Abraham. As Hagar was wandering the desert with her young son, Ishmael, they reached Mecca nearly dead of thirst. While Hagar was looking for water between two hills, Ishmael waited in the shade of a tree. Then, as Ishmael cried out with thirst, small bubbles under his feet became a stream of sweet, flowing water. The place where the water is believed to have appeared first is known as the well of Zemzem, which still gives water today.

The legend doesn't end there, however. Abraham supposedly made a visit to Zemzem to offer his son as a sacrifice. According to this legend, of course, that son was Ishmael—in the Bible, the son of sacrifice was Isaac and the place of sacrifice was Mount Morah.

When Abraham was stopped from sacrificing Ishmael, the legend explains, Abraham and Ishmael together built the Kaaba at God's command.

Jews who lived in Arabia at the time the Kaaba was built refused to participate in the pagan worship offered there, refuting the story as myth by claiming that Abraham never came as far south as Mecca.

The Kabba nonetheless became the focal point of early religious rituals.

Strong Historical Resistance to the Gospel

Two factors combined to make Arabia unusually resistant to the spread of the Christian Gospel.

First, the idolatry practiced in Mecca was a compromise with Judaism. Enough legends had been instilled into the people's minds to steel them against Christianity. The tenets of Judaism were very familiar to the Arabians, and to some extent, the worship at the Kaaba was founded on Jewish patriarchal traditions.

Second, Arabian Christianity in the seventh century was rather corrupt, beset by a number of heresies and schisms regarding the nature of Christ. The New Testament was respected as a literary document, and at times revered for its claim to be the revealed Word of God, but the few Christians in Arabia had embraced a decrepit form of Christianity and for the most part, Christianity had no appeal to the people there.

In many ways, the spiritual soil of Arabia was "ready" for a religious rebirth—the potential for a transformation of religious consciousness existed, but it needed molding and shaping. In a cave at the foot of Mount Hira near Mecca, a man from the tribe of Quaraish named Ibn Abd Allah stepped into this religious vacuum in 610 A.D. and emerged with a vision and a message. That man is better known as Muhammad.

I have no doubt that had Muhammad embraced genuine Christian truth as it was being experienced in Europe and elsewhere, we would likely have in Christian history a "Saint Muhammad"—or perhaps more likely "Muhammad the Martyr"—as the person who laid the foundation stone of the Arabian church.

The Supreme Prophet of Islam

Islam begins and ends with a two-fold proclamation: "There is no god but God (Allah), and Muhammad is the Messenger (Prophet) of God." To understand the first part of that confession, we must understand the nature of the Messenger.

Who was Muhammad?

Born in Mecca in the autumn of 570 A.D., Muhammad was given his name by his mother and his grandfather. The name is rare among Arabs. It means "highly praised." His father, a trader named Abdullah, died before Muhammad was born. According to the custom of Meccan aristocracy, the infant Muhammad was sent to the desert to be wet-nursed by a Bedouin mother. Muhammad spent most of his childhood years with this nurse, Halima, among the Beni Saad tribesmen.

At age five Muhammad was sent back to his mother, but she subsequently became ill and died. His care then became the responsibility of Abdul Muttelib, his grandfather. Abdul Muttelib loved Muhammad devotedly, but unfortunately, he too died soon after Muhammad's arrival. Guardianship of the child went to Abu Talib, Muhammad's uncle.

At age twelve Muhammad took his first business trip to Syria with Abu Talib. The journey took several months and was filled with a multitude of rich experiences that were not wasted on the young Muhammad. During the journey, Muhammad came into contact with both Jewish settlements and Christians in Syria. He no doubt saw churches, crosses, and the images and symbols of the Christian faith.

Muhammad was also exposed to still another custom that was no doubt influential in his life. In Mecca during the seventh century, both Jewish and Christian poets and theologians recited their poetry or preached the essence of their faith to the crowds that attended annual "fairs" in the city. These recitations did not give Muhammad a comprehensive or deep understanding of either religion—only a smattering of information. Muhammad's later writings reveal far more familiarity with Judaism than with Christianity, probably because Judaism was more prominent in the area. One thing must have been very clear, however—Christians and Jews regarded each other with great disdain, and both Christians and Jews spurned the Arab tribes as heathens who were destined to receive the wrath of an offended God.

Little else is known about Muhammad's early years. Like other young men, he probably tended sheep and goats in the neighboring hills and valleys. Authorities agree that he was respected for his thoughtful nature and his integrity. He was nicknamed al-Amin, "the trustworthy." He appears to have lived a quiet, peaceful life with the family of Abu Talib.

At age twenty-five, while traveling the same route he had trekked earlier with his uncle, Muhammad led a caravan expedition to Syria for a widow named Khadija. This time, Muhammad lost no time delving into the practices of the Syrian Christians and conversing with the monks and clergy he met. Later, in writing the Koran, he spoke of them with respect and even praise. He had no sympathy, however, for their doctrine—it is apparent in his writings that he also had little genuine understanding of the true teachings of Christ.

Major stumbling points for Muhammad were the role of Mary and the divinity of Jesus. Sir William Muir wrote:

> Instead of the simple message of the Gospel as a revelation of God reconciling mankind unto Himself through His son, the sacred dogma of the trinity was forced upon the traveler with...offensive zeal...and the worship of Mary was exhibited in so gross a form as to leave the impression in Muhammad's mind that she was held to be a goddess if not the third person of the

trinity. (Sir William Muir, *The Life of Mohammed* [Edinburgh: John Grant, 1923], 22)

The ancient Arab pagans held to a belief that the gods could have sexual intercourse with human women, producing children called the sons of God. Muhammad rejected that pagan belief, but in turn, also rejected the idea that God could father a child from a human woman. The end result was that Muhammad refused to call Jesus the Son of God, choosing instead to call Him the son of Mary.

Upon his return from this commercial venture, which proved to be very successful financially, Muhammad married Khadija. She was fifteen years older than Muhammad and had been married twice before. She remained his only wife as long as she lived and she bore Muhammad two sons and a daughter. After her death, Muhammad took nine other wives and still more concubines.

A Mid-Life Vision in a Cave. As he approached forty, Muhammad spent more and more time pondering the age-old question, "What is truth?" His soul was perplexed, and he was equally perplexed at the social injustice he saw among the clans in his own tribe.

Muhammad's clan was the poorer of two main clans in the Quaraish tribe. He was distressed to watch the rival clan grow rich and strong, even as his own grew weaker. One of his aims was to create a more just social system that would protect the poor, the widows and orphans, and would replace the existing system in which the strong abused the weak.

Troubled in spirit, Muhammad frequently resorted to the countryside near Mecca to meditate in solitude. His favorite spot was a cave about two or three miles to the north of the city.

According to the account of Ibn Ishaq, who was the first biographer of Muhammad, the future prophet was sound asleep when the angel Gabriel appeared and commanded, "Recite!"

Startled and afraid, Muhammad asked, "What shall I recite?" Immediately he felt his throat tighten as if the angel had grabbed his neck and was choking him.

"Recite!" the angel again commanded.

Muhammad again felt the angel's grip.

A third time the angel commanded, "Recite! Recite in the name of the Lord, the Creator who created man from a clot of blood! Recite! Your Lord is most gracious. It is he who has taught man by the pen that which he does not know."

Muhammad felt inspired to preach the word of "Allah," his name for the Creator, and the first verses of the Koran were revealed to him. That first section of the Koran has a title that literally means "recitation."

Muhammad's own account of his revelation is worth noting. He said,

> Inspiration cometh in one of two ways; sometimes Gabriel communicateth the revelation to me, as one man to another, and this is easy; at other times, it is like the ringing of a bell, penetrating my very heart, and rending me; and this it is which afflicteth me the most. (Muir, *The Life of Mohammed.*)

Muhammad returned from this experience in the cave and told Khadija that God had commissioned him to preach. She lost no time in consulting her *hanif* kinsman, a holy man who listened to the story and unhesitatingly declared that Muhammad had been chosen, like Moses, to receive divine inspiration and to be the prophet of his people. As long as Khadija lived, she gave unfailing support to Muhammad even though many in Mecca did not want to hear his message.

The Meccans rejected Muhammad initially for one main reason—he was illiterate. Muhammad turned this to his advantage, however, by stating that his illiteracy substantiated his claim to have received his revelations directly from Allah.

Muslims through the centuries have regarded Muhammad's vision as sacred and his recitation as a "miraculous act" of God. Muhammad himself, however, worked no miracles. Again, Muhammad turned this to his advantage. He stressed his "ordinary humanity" as a prophet. Muslims, as a result, take pride in the fact that they do not call themselves Muhammadans, because such a term would imply that they worship Muhammad—as Christians worship Christ.

Even before his first revelation, Muhammad had a reputation for being a wise and saintly man. An example of his wisdom is expressed in a major legend of Islam. According to this legend, Muhammad looked out from his balcony one day to see members of four clans engaged in a dispute as to who would carry the

Black Stone, which the pagan Arabs regarded as sacred, to its new niche in the Kaaba. Muhammad successfully resolved the argument to everyone's satisfaction by proposing a compromise. He instructed each tribe to lift one corner of a blanket upon which he placed the meteorite, and he personally set the Black Stone in its resting place, where it remains today.

During the period after his initial revelation and recitation, Muhammad received no further messages from God. He became fearful and depressed, even to the point of considering suicide. Accounts are a bit confused. This period is thought to have lasted anywhere from six months to three years. Let it suffice that Muhammad went through a period in which he himself was confused and uncertain of himself and his mission.

Emergence on a Broader Public Platform. By the time he was forty-four, Muhammad had emerged from both personal doubt and public obscurity. He asserted unequivocally that he was ordained a prophet with a commission to the people of Arabia. He recited his warnings, exhortations, and messages as coming directly from God. He taught that Allah was the one God and that men must thank him for their existence and worship him only. He preached equality before God and justice among men and warned that because man's destiny was in God's hands, a Day of Judgment was coming for all men.

Muhammad's wife Khadija was his first convert, followed by his slave Zaid, whom he later adopted as his son. Then followed two of his most trusted friends, Abu Bakr and Umar, who later succeeded him as leaders of the Muslim movement. In Mecca, however, Muhammad met with stiff opposition from his own tribe, which refused to acknowledge him as a prophet and refused to give up idol worship.

The Jews in the area, however, did *not* oppose Muhammad as much as his own tribesmen did. He developed a close relationship with the Jews, some of whom acknowledged him as a prophet, others as the messiah descended from Abraham. The majority of Jews took a "wait and see" policy. Perhaps to gain their favor, perhaps a result of their influence, Muhammad incorporated into his new religion many Jewish traditions and a number of Old Testament stories. The Koran includes the story of Abraham and Ishmael, Hagar and Ishmael, stories about Joseph and Jacob, and the account of the destruction of Sodom and

Gomorrah. In the Koran, these stories are usually mixed with other extra biblical stories, myths, and legends.

Migration to Medina. Muhammad's attempts to win the hearts of the Meccans proved frustrating and unsuccessful. Discouraged, Muhammad and his followers moved to Medina in a mass migration known in Islamic history as the *hijra*. In Medina, Muhammad struck a more responsive chord in the people's hearts. The city had a large community of Jews—in fact, three of the five tribes living in the city were Jewish. The Jews had endlessly threatened the Arab tribes in the area with warnings that the coming messiah would inflict revenge upon them for the injustices they committed. The population was ripe to accept Muhammad's message—as a whole, the people of Medina were far more prepared to accept a monotheistic religion than were the more worldly Meccans.

It was in Medina that Muhammad successfully brought Jews and pagans together under the banner of Allah. He managed to please the Jews by adopting some of their religious rites. The Jewish Day of Atonement became the Muslim fast day of Ashura. Prayer was increased from two to three times (later to five times) daily to accommodate the Jewish morning, midday, and evening prayers. Muslims held a public service, such as the Jews had in their synagogues. The Muslims declared Friday to be their holy day, accommodating the fact that the Jews already began their Sabbath at sundown on Friday. And, Muhammad adopted the Jewish call to prayer. Instead of using the trumpet of the Jews, however, he used a human prayer-caller (*muezzin*).

Later, when Jews opposed and rejected Muhammad's message, he became both disappointed and angered, and he accused the Jews of rejecting the truth and claimed Jewish property for his own private property. By the time he left Medina, Muslim Arabs had gained control of the city—the two Arab tribes that had lost virtually everything to the Jews had been restored to dignity and power.

Muhammad never showed an interest in courting Christians to his cause, or in adopting Christian rituals and beliefs. Nor did he have the same opportunity to learn its history and doctrines. Tradition holds that shortly after Muhammad's initial revelation, Khadija's cousin, Waraqa ibn Naufal—a Christian scholar—translated portions of the New Testament into Hebrew and Arabic. Waraqa was tutoring Muhammad in the Christian faith, but after a short time, Waraqa died. Some attribute

Muhammad's "confused period" to Muhammad's struggle with what Waraqa had taught him.

For whatever reasons, Muhammad had a generally favorable attitude toward Christianity—his relationship with the few Christians living on the Arabian Peninsula was not embittered or hostile, which became the hallmarks of his relationship with the Jews. At the same time, Muhammad's relationship with the Christian faith never advanced significantly beyond the point at which it is described in the Koran.

Progression in Teachings. Muhammad's overall teachings followed this progression: He began by warning and seeking to reform the pagan society of the Arabian peninsula, asking people to turn to the true God, the God of Abraham. Next, he equated his revelation with that of Judaism and Christianity, perceiving himself to be on equal footing with Moses and Jesus. And finally, he saw himself and his message as the final word of God that superseded both Judaism and Christianity. Muhammad believed that because Jews and Christians had moved away from God's intended purposes, God had sent him to proclaim the ultimate revelation, and his teachings rose triumphant over both the Law and the Gospel.

In the end, Muhammad claimed that Islam was the universal faith—a faith that started with Abraham (whom Muhammad called the "first Muslim"). At the same time, he was strict in his belief that the new message of Allah was announced in the Arabic language and intended for Arabs, who henceforth would have a prophet and a holy book of their own.

To Muhammad, the Jew was to follow the Law and the Christian was to hold fast to the Gospel. Both Jew and Christian were to admit the apostleship of Muhammad and the authority of the Koran as being equal to their own respective prophets, teachers, and writings. The Koran states:

> Say: O People of the Book! Ye do not stand upon any sure ground until you observe both the Torah and the Gospel as well as that which has been now sent down unto you from your Lord (Koran, 5:68)

The Jewish Response. How did Jews on the Arabian Peninsula respond to Muhammad? For a short time the Jews remained on fairly cordial terms with their new ally—this stance lasted as long as Muhammad saw his mission as a protest against error and superstition. As Islam became more exclusive and demanded priority status, Jews backed away quickly. By the time he began his farewell pilgrimage, Muhammad barred Christians and Jews from visiting the Kaaba and by "divine command" declared their continued exclusion until they confessed the supremacy of Islam or consented to pay tribute.

Muhammad initially used the ancient legend about Abraham and Ishmael to legitimize his new religion. He argued that Islam's relationship to Abraham made Islam the equal of Judaism and Christianity. Later in his life, of course, he revised this claim, stating that his revelation superseded both Judaism and Christianity and had become the final revelation of God.

Death of the Prophet. When Muhammad was sixty-three, and Islam was only twenty years old, the self-proclaimed "apostle of God" fell ill with a sudden fever and died. As the news of his death spread, new Muslims were seized with panic and confusion. Abu Bakr, Muhammad's close friend and later the first Islamic caliph (successor of the Prophet), declared to Muhammad's distraught followers, "Whichever of you worships Muhammad, know that Muhammad is dead. But which of you worships God, know that God is alive and does not die." He then quoted a verse from the Koran that gains even greater significant with the hindsight of history: "Muhammad is a Prophet only; there have been Prophets before him. If he dies or is slain, will ye turn back?"

The Koran: Supreme Book of Islam

Muslims believe God has spoken to man throughout the ages, and specifically, to those called prophets. Muslims regard Muhammad as the "final" prophet of God. Islam acknowledges other prophets before Muhammad's time—including the great figures of the Old and New Testaments such as Abraham, Moses, David, and Jesus—but Islam contends that God gave Muhammad the complete revelation of the final divine truth. This ultimate knowledge of God is only found in the pages of the Koran, the collection of Muhammad's proclamations that his followers memorized and recorded. It is through Muhammad that Allah allegedly made known the fullness of his laws and spelled out precisely what he expects from man morally, ethically, and religiously.

Islam requires that the Koran be obeyed *literally*. The thinking is this: The Koran is explicit and literal; man has no alternative but to obey the Koran literally to be in compliance with God's rules. The objection of many who are considered Islamic extremists today is that the Koran has been interpreted figuratively, and that this represents a compromise with Western godlessness. Islam contends that all mankind should seek to know Allah's will as revealed in the Koran, and then be in total submission to Allah's will.

The enforcement of what is perceived to be God's law on earth is of paramount importance to zealous Muslims. The *enforcement* of the Koran is at the root of the regimes of those who call themselves Islamic fundamentalists. Such fundamentalists are growing in number worldwide, and they have especially strong movements in Egypt, Pakistan, Syria, Iran, and among the Palestinian people in Israel. This zeal to enforce the Koran was the core of the Taliban's hold on the people of Afghanistan. Those who see themselves as being in a position to enforce the Koran are often ruthless. The Ayatollah Khomeini, for example, did not spare the lives of some of his closest friends who disagreed with his convictions about what form an Islamic government should take to fulfill the Koran's demands.

Moderates, who should perhaps be termed "less zealous" Muslims, have good reason to be concerned when zealous Muslims take over political control. Much of the freedom they enjoy, including freedom to interpret the Koran, is stripped away.

The concern for those who are *not* Muslims should be even greater since the Koran has *explicit* rules for dealing with non-Muslims, and if those rules are interpreted literally and strictly, the lives of all non-Muslims are subject to assault. (This is explained in greater detail in a later chapter.)

The Koran has 114 suras or chapters, starting with the longest and ending with the shortest. The order of the suras is not in any historical or chronological order—and therefore it is impossible to determine at what stage in Muhammad's life these "revelations" were given to him. They are simply put in order of length, beginning with the longest and moving toward the shortest.

Muhammad *spoke* his revelations and his literate followers wrote the revelation on whatever they could find to write upon—everything from leaves to dried bones, to scraps of parchment.

A number of Muslim scholars have attempted to put events in the Koran in something of a chronological order. One Muslim scholar, Ibn-Ishaq, gives this order: Creation, Adam and Eve, Noah and his offspring, Hud, Salih, Abraham, Lot, Job, Shu-ayb, Joseph, Moses, Ezekiel, Elijah, Elisha, Samuel, David, Solomon, Sheba, Isaiah, al-Khidr, Daniel, Hananiah, Azariah, Mishael and Ezra, Alexander, Zecharia and John, the family of Imran and Jesus, son of Mary; the Companion of the Cave, Jonah, the Three Messengers, Samson, and George.

Christians certainly are quick to note that many of these so-called prophets from the Koran are not mentioned in either Old or New Testament texts, and that those that *are* mentioned are vastly out of order in history.

Due to the fact that Muhammad had a very sketchy knowledge of the Bible you will find that the Koran differs significantly from the Bible in the relating to the facts of various stories. Here are just a few of the differences:

- In the Koran, one of Noah's sons separated himself from the rest of the family and died in the floodwaters—the ark later came to rest on Mount Judi. (11:32–48) In the Bible, all in Noah's family were spared, and the ark came to rest on Mount Ararat. (Gen. 7:1–13 and 8:4)

- In the Koran, Abraham dwelt in a "valley without cultivation" by the Kabah. (14:37) This valley is thought to have been the Meccan valley. In the Bible, Abraham dwelt in Hebron. (Gen. 13:18)

- In the Koran, the *wife* of Pharaoh plucked Moses from the river, saying, "It may be that he will be of use to us." (28:8–9) In the Bible, the daughter of Pharaoh took Moses from the river, sparing his life out of compassion. (Ex. 2)

- In the Koran, the first miracle assigned to Jesus is the making of a clay bird and then breathing life into it so it became a living bird. (3:49) In the Bible, the first miracle of Jesus is the turning of water into wine at Cana. (John 2:11)

- In the Koran, Zechariah is speechless for three nights. (3:38–41 and 19:16–34) In the Bible, he is mute from the time the angel speaks to him until after John (the Baptist) is born. (Luke 1)

- In the Koran, Jesus was not crucified, only "so it was made to appear to them." (4:157) In the Bible, Jesus was crucified, died, and was buried. (Matt 17, Mark 15, Luke 23, John 19)

- The Koran says of Jesus: "Christ, the son of Mary, was no more than a messenger." (5:75) The Bible presents Jesus this way: "In the past God spoke to our forefathers through the prophets at many times and in various ways, but in these last days he has spoken to us by his Son, whom he appointed heir of all things, and through whom he made the universe. The Son is the radiance of God's glory and the exact representation of his being, sustaining all things by his powerful word. After he had provided purification for sins, he sat down at the right hand of the Majesty in heaven." (Heb. 1:1–3)

- The Koran says that "Allah loveth not those who reject Faith" and "Allah loveth not those who do wrong." (3:32,57) The Bible says that God "so loved the world that he gave his one and only Son, that whoever believes in him shall not perish but have eternal life" (John 3:16) and that "while we were still sinners, Christ died for us." (Rom. 5:8)

- The Koran says to men that they are to be the "protectors and maintainers of women" but also gives men these rights if they fear their wives are disloyal or show ill conduct: "admonish them (first), (next) refuse to share their beds, (and last) beat them lightly." (4:34) The Koran also says to husbands, "Your wives are as a tilth [a piece of farmland] unto you so approach your tilth when or how you will." (2:223) The Bible says, "Husbands, love your wives, just as Christ loved the church and gave himself up for her" and "Husbands, in the same way be considerate as you live with your wives, and treat them with respect as the weaker partner and as heirs with you of the gracious gift of life." (Eph. 5:25–28 and 1 Pet. 3:7)

- The Koran says about man's relationship to God: "(Both) the Jews and the Christians say: 'We are sons of Allah, and His beloved,' Say: 'Why then doth He punish you for your sins? Nay, ye are but men—of the men He hath created: He forgiveth whom He pleaseth, and he punisheth whom He pleaseth: and to Allah belongeth the dominion of the heavens and the earth, and all that is between: and unto Him is the final goal (of all). (5:18) The Bible holds out, "We are children of God, and what we will be has not yet been made known. But we know that when he appears, we shall be like him, for we shall see him as he is." (1 John 3:2)

A Book Largely Unread. Muslims as a whole have not read their own holy book. One man who converted from Islam to Christianity has written,

I have more knowledge of the Koran now as a Christian than I ever had as a fanatical Muslim. Of all the Muslims I knew, only a handful had some knowledge of the Koran. Even today when I confront many fanatical Muslims with strange revelations of Muhammad in the Koran, they are unaware these verses are in the book. (Reza F. Safa, *Inside Islam: Exposing and Reaching the World of Islam* [Lake Mary, FL: Charisma House, 1996] 70)

There are several reasons that Muslims have not and do not read the Koran.

First, the rate of illiteracy among Muslims is very high. In some Muslim nations in Asia and Africa, seventy-five to eighty-five percent of the people cannot read or write.

Second, many Muslims are too poor to own a copy of the Koran for themselves. The book has not been widely published or circulated to the poor, in part because the reading of the Koran is not emphasized as a spiritual discipline.

Third, Muslims believe that the Koran must be read in Arabic, which is spoken only by Arab Muslims. In fact, translations into languages other than Arabic are not considered to be the genuine Koran, but a mere "interpretation" of the Koran.

Only about 140 to 200 million Muslims live in the twenty-two Arab-speaking nations of the world. (That figure represents about fifteen to twenty percent of the world's population of Muslims.) In all, of the more than one billion people who call themselves Muslims, some eight hundred million of them cannot read, write, or speak Arabic.

Even those who can read Arabic rarely read the Koran. Many consider the language too "poetic" or very difficult to understand.

If Muslims do not read the Koran, how do they know what the Koran teaches? They know only the "interpretation" given to the Koran by their religious leaders. Many Muslims know little beyond the five pillars of Islam (explained in a later chapter) and the traditional way of keeping those customs in their own culture. Most Muslims have not been challenged to read the Koran and they feel no *need* to read it.

An Opinion the Bible Has Been Corrupted. There is little to be gained from arguing the accuracy of the Bible and the Koran with a Muslim since Muslims almost universally believe that the Bible has been corrupted or altered. This argument is routinely taught in Islam and is based, in part, on the fact that Jesus did not write or dictate the Gospels personally.

Many believe the Gospel accounts have been "elaborated upon" or "edited" in the last two thousand years. For example, there is a strong teaching that when Jesus spoke of sending another "Comforter" to the people after He left the earth, Jesus meant Muhammad, not the Holy Spirit. Some have gone so far as to argue that the Bible was "edited" to insert references to the Holy Spirit—even though this would have entailed universal and simultaneous editing of more than two hundred thousand handwritten documents in circulation around the world by the time Muhammad was born.

A Command to Read the Gospel. Interestingly, even as modern-day Islam rejects the Gospel accounts as corrupt, the Koran itself *commands* Muslims to read the *Injeil*, the Gospel accounts of

Jesus. Few Muslims are aware of this command, and are equally unaware of these statements in the Koran:

- "Say ye: 'We believe in God, and the revelation given to us, and to Abraham, Ishmael, Isaac, Jacob, and the Tribes, and in that given to Moses and to Jesus, and that given to all the prophets from their Lord. We make no distinctions between one and another of them." (2:136)

- if thou wert in doubt as to what we have revealed to thee, then ask those who were reading the Book from before thee." (10:94) The Book refers to the Bible.

- Jesus is called Muhammad's "Lord" (89:22) and the Truth (2:91) Jesus is also described as the "Word of God" (3:45, 4:171) and a "Spirit Proceeding forth from God" (4:171).

A Total "Culture"—Ideally Arabic

Muhammad not only espoused a new religious doctrine—he formed a *new religious society*. Islam is far more than a religion. It is total way of thinking, feeling, and responding to all of life. It is a culture.

To ensure his political preeminence, Muhammad spoke about rewards—economic and spiritual—that would go to those who embraced his espoused doctrine and moral code. He declared, "Paradise is the reward for those who die in the way of God and the booty is the reward of those who survive the war." Presumably this war is the war against non-Muslims.

Throughout the Koran, Muhammad developed a form of theocratic government pertinent to all departments of life. He began with the conduct of dissidents, the treatment of allies, the formation of treaties, and other political matters. Later, elements of a code of conduct and moral law were introduced.

The *Hadith* stands next to the Koran in the writings of Islam. The *Hadith* is a collection of Islamic traditions including sayings and deeds of Muhammad as heard by his contemporaries, first, second, and third hand. Many of the sayings elaborate on the teachings of the Koran. A great many Muslims cannot differentiate Hadith from Koran—they do not know what Muhammad "recited" and what others *say* he said or did.

Toward the end of his life, Muhammad began to clarify his own aspirations as to the future spread of Islam. He made a silver seal engraved with the words "Muhammad the apostle of God" and sent four simultaneous messages bearing this stamp to the rulers of Egypt, Abyssinia, Syria, and Persia. He urged them to forsake their idols and to believe the true universal faith of God's message given through him, God's messenger.

In launching this outward appeal to other nations, the culture of Islam was also being "exported." That culture was not only Islamic, but also Arabic.

Throughout the Muslim world, Arab culture is still considered by many to be the ideal expression of Islam. The vast majority of OPEC members are Muslim nations—Venezuela and Nigeria are the only two notable exceptions—and the vast majority of Muslim nations are Arabic in culture.

Algeria's Ben Bella once said, "I cannot see Arab culture separate from Islamic culture. I honestly would not understand the meaning of Arab culture if it were not first and foremost Islamic."

This alignment between the Arab culture and Islam runs extremely deep in the hearts and minds of the Arab people. It is one of the foremost reasons that fanatic Muslims are deeply angered when their Arab countrymen adopt certain Western cultural behaviors—from modes of dress to preferred Western styles of entertainment. To the Arab Islamic mind, Western lifestyle is inherently anti-Islamic, and therefore, should be anathema to Arabs. Stated another way, Western clothing is not Arabic and therefore, it cannot be Islamic.

Many have asked me why the Muslims are so adamant about head coverings (burkah and chador for women, turban-style cloth head coverings for men). The answer: these head coverings were popular in the Arabic culture for thousands of years, largely as a means of withstanding the blowing desert sands. When Islam became the religion of Arabia, so the dress of Arabia became an expression of Islam. It doesn't matter if a person lives in the cold, high-mountain regions of Afghanistan or the jungle conditions of central Africa, to be a Muslim means to dress like Arabs!

Muhammad's goal, of course, was to create a society in which religion encompassed all aspects of the culture—from dress to music to entertainment to education. The goal of Islamic leaders even today is the complete blend of religion and culture, and generally speaking, that culture is Arabic.

23

Chapter Three

ARE JEHOVAH AND ALLAH THE SAME GOD?

As stated in the previous chapter, the confession of faith for Muslims is a brief eight-word statement: "There is no god but Allah, and Muhammad is the Messenger of God." This one line sums up the central belief of the world's Muslims. It also establishes what appears to be common ground between Islam and other religions that proclaim the existence of one, sovereign God.

Like Judaism and Christianity, the older religions that preceded and influenced it, Islam is monotheistic. It is also a "revealed" religion—in other words, a religion in which the adherents believe the tenets of the religion came by direct revelation from God.

But is Jehovah—the God of Judaism and Christianity—the same as Allah? How does Islam vary from biblical doctrine? What do Muslims believe about the nature of God and the nature of man? What do they believe about how God and man are to relate? These are vitally important questions to ask, and unfortunately, questions the vast majority of people in the West have never asked.

Allah and Jehovah Are Very Different in Character

Monotheism is pivotal to Islamic doctrine. The Koran does not attempt to prove or argue the existence of Allah; it proclaims his existence as a matter of fact.

The Koran gives ninety-nine attributes of Allah. These are called the "most Beautiful Names." Many are ones with which Christians would readily agree: all-powerful, Creator, the Merciful, the Compassionate. The essence of Allah, however, is power—power overrides all his other attributes. The word Islam itself means "submission to God." Nothing less than total surrender of man's life is owed to the all-knowing, all-powerful Allah.

Allah is removed, aloof, and distant. He is considered to be neither wholly a spirit nor a physical entity, but an entirely separate form of creation. Jehovah, in contrast, has always been portrayed as seeking a relationship with mankind. He walked and talked with Adam and Eve in the Garden of Eden. He sought to have a relationship marked by this definition, "You will be My people and I will be Your God."

The Koran presents Allah as "far," transcendent only. As a Muslim theologian has stated, "He remains hidden forever." The Bible presents Jehovah as "drawing near," "coming down," and "seeking after" man. The first question we find in the Bible is God calling to Adam and Eve, "Where are you?" (Gen. 3:9) In the Bible, it is man who is portrayed as hiding from God, not God hidden in secrecy from mankind.

Although Allah is considered supremely powerful, he requires that his name be avenged. Allah requires that man seek his own justice and that the faithful require the submission of others to Allah. Jehovah does not make these demands. Rather than seek to avenge God, the Israelites turned to Jehovah to avenge them! Muslims are routinely called to "fight" for Allah and for Allah's will to be established among the people. Jews throughout their history asked Jehovah to fight on their behalf.

Christians also look to God to fight on their behalf and provide justice for them. As they await His actions on their behalf, they are called to pray for their enemies, do good to them, and "turn the other cheek" when they are wrongly treated.

The Name *Allah*. *Allah* is a pre-Islamic name. It corresponds to the Babylonian name *Bel* (Baal). (*Encyclopedia of Religion*, ed. Paul Meagher, Thomas O'Brian, Consuela Aherne [Washington, D.C.: Corpus Publisher, 1979, I:117]) According to Middle East scholar E. M. Wherry, in pre-Islamic times both Allah-worship and Baal-worship involved worship of the sun, the moon, and the stars—in scholarly terms, they were "astral" religions. The crescent moon, which was the symbol of pagan moon worship, is also the symbol of Islam. It is printed on the flags of many Islamic countries and placed on top of minarets and mosques. (E.M. Wherry, *A Comprehensive Commentary on the Quran* [Ornabruck, Germany: Otto Zeller Verlag, 1973], 36)

A Revealed Plan or a Revealed Identity? In Islam, the angel Gabriel supposedly was sent to reveal Allah's will to Muhammad. Muhammad was not given insight into the nature, character, personality, or identity of God—he was given God's designated plan that man was commissioned to implement. Jehovah God, in contrast, revealed Himself to Abraham, whom He called friend. He conversed with Moses, giving Moses His name and showing Himself to Moses (although not face to face). We read repeatedly in the Bible, "Thus saith the Lord," not just to one prophet through an angel, but directly to the prophets. The God of the Bible has revealed Himself through the giving of various names that describe His character, His attributes, and His identity.

Faith in the Truth. . . But Which Truth?

Muslim and Christians disagree as to how people should *relate* to God. Both Islam and Christianity call for people to accept "by faith" what they assert has been revealed by God. There is no disagreement about the need for faith. There is vast disagreement, however, when it comes to what has been revealed. The claims to divine truth rival each other.

Islam contends that the ultimate truth was revealed by Allah to Muhammad. They strongly contend that the Bible in its present form is corrupt and that only the Koran contains the true divine message.

Christians contend that the ultimate truth was *evident* in the life of Jesus Christ, who said of Himself, "I am the way and the truth and the life. No one comes to the Father except through me." (John 14:6) Jesus revealed *God's* truth by His life as the incarnate Son (full expression) of God.

A Very Different Concept of Sin

Much of what the Koran says about the practice of sin sounds a great deal like what the Bible says. The Koran uses several words for sin—behind them all is the idea of failing to come up to the standards set by God.

Since Islam contends that man was created for the service of Allah, and that service includes absolute obedience to what Allah has commanded, the root of sin lies in man's prideful opposition to God's will. Man is prone to wrong actions because he is weak. Therefore, it is up to man to choose to be strong and to do good works. If he does so, his good works will ward off evil. The Koran teaches, "Surely good deeds take away evil deeds." (11:14)

Muslims believe Allah has given to all people the ability to obey. Therefore, mankind only needs to be guided into obedience. The exertion of *will* is the expression of faith.

The Koran does not consider the original sin to have totally depraved mankind. Islam, therefore, has no overall doctrine of a "sin nature." The Koran reveals that Muhammad himself had no deep conviction concerning sin, and he did not demand that believers experience any such conviction. Rather, Islam puts forth ideas about specific wrongdoing—classifying various misdeeds as being great or small for the purpose of determining the degree of punishment these misdeeds deserve.

"Great sins"—*kabira*—include things such as murder, adultery, disobeying God, disobeying one's parents, drinking to excess, practicing usury, neglecting Friday prayers, not keeping the fast of Ramadan, forgetting the Koran after reading it, swearing falsely or by any other name than that of Allah, performing magic, gambling, dancing, or shaving the beard. Such sins can be forgiven only after repentant deeds. By the way, adultery and fornication are often labeled as "temporary marriage" rather than sin. (4:3–34)

"Little sins"—*saghira*—include lying, deception, anger, and lust. Sins of this class are easily forgiven if the greater sins are avoided, and if some compensatory good actions are performed. A lie may be good "as long as it helps someone."

The sin that surpasses all others in Islam is *shirk*, the association of other deities with Allah. This is unpardonable. According to tradition, Muhammad was asked to identify the greatest sin and he said it was polytheism, the worship of more than one deity. Christians, of course, fall into this from the perspective of Islam, since Muslims regard Christians as believing in three gods (the Trinity) rather than one God. And, by the way, this is all the justification Muslims need to wage a holy war on Christians—and to seek to convert, conquer, or eliminate them as unbelievers who have corrupted the true faith of Allah.

The Muslims view of Allah is that of an elderly, cherubic Arab who is always happy when people obey him and furiously angry when they disobey—and he rewards or punishes them according to his happiness or anger. To the faithful, Allah is Lord of Bounty, but like a benevolent dictator, he insists on total compliance with his laws. This is one of the reasons why perhaps Islamic nations are not democracies, with the exception of Turkey. Muslims' view of Allah is tied up with their view of any ruler, whether he be monarch or dictator. The concept of "ruler" is closely associated with the concept of power, pleasure expressed toward obedient subjects and ruthless displeasure expressed toward disobedient subjects.

Even so, Muslims believe Allah can be merciful if he chooses. He accepts repentance and forgives faults and shortcomings. The opening words of each chapter of the Koran are these: "In the name of God, the merciful." Muslims believe that every word and every accent in the Koran reveal the mercies of God.

The Koran teaches that forgiveness has to be *sought* because Allah is all-knowing (another similarity with the Bible). Allah sees the secrets of the heart—nothing escapes his notice. It is Allah's *maghfera* ("forgiveness") that preserves a person from being punished. The Koran proclaims repeatedly that Allah forgives sins, but it is important to remember this distinction: forgiveness is purely the prerogative of Allah. There is no means by which a human being can know with certainty that he has been forgiven—other than a possible inference that since nothing bad has happened to him, he must have been forgiven.

There is no means for atoning for the sins of man. There are no sacrifices, such as in Judaism. There is no atoning blood of Christ to cover the sins of the believer once and for all. There is, therefore, no means of determining when, how, or with what results a person is forgiven.

Even though he is addressed as "merciful," Allah remains a stern, unbending figure who is just as likely to dispense forgiveness "on a whim" as by "will."

In summary, Allah provides no means for man to be cleansed of sin, because Islam does not recognize that man needs such cleansing. Judaism and Christianity disagree sharply—man has a sin nature from birth and sin must be cleansed. For the Jews, Jehovah provided a means of atonement through the blood sacrifices of the Mosaic Law. For the Christian, the ultimate atoning sacrifice was Jesus' death on the Cross.

A Very Different Approach to Jesus

The incarnation of Christ is a major stumbling block for Muslims. Christians believe that Jesus is God's Son..."God in the flesh". . . God having taken human form to dwell among mankind. Muslims cannot accept this.

Muhammad, influenced by the polytheistic environment of pre-Islamic Arabia, thought Christians believed God had "married" a human woman and produced a son by her. That's what much of polytheism is all about—the "gods" marrying human beings and producing offspring, many of which seem to have supernatural powers. Very rightly, Muhammad rejected this as a pagan belief. However, Muhammad also mistakenly thought Christians believed the Trinity was composed of Jesus, God, and Mary! The various heresies surrounding the worship of Mary at the time of Muhammad were abundant—it is not too difficult to see how Muhammad concluded that Christians worshiped more than one God.

Islam contends that Jesus, called Isa in the Koran, was a prophet of God. The religion accepts Jesus' miracles. Christians have special status in Islam as "People of the Book." But Muslims do *not* believe Jesus was divine.

Islam not only denies that Jesus is the Son of God, but it pronounces a curse on all who confess Jesus to be the Christ, the

Son of God, and the Lord worthy to be followed. The Koran says:

> The Jews call "Uzayr [a person of unknown identity] a son of God," and the Christians call "Christ the Son of God." That is a saying from their mouth; (in this) they but imitate what the Unbelievers of the old used to say. Allah's curse be on them: how they are deluded away from the Truth." (9:30)

A "curse" in Islam is tantamount to a death sentence.

Islam and the Cross. The purpose for the Cross eludes Muslims because they see no need for a sacrifice for sin. Furthermore, substitutionary atonement is a primitive and savage idea to the Muslim mind. Muslims do not abhor the shedding of blood, but they vehemently reject virtue in dying for someone else. Muslims die for the sake of the advancement of Islam, but not for the sake of other Muslims. Muslims cannot comprehend what to Christians is the highest expression of love—a love that takes the consequences of sin upon itself and finds its meaning in forgiveness and redemption.

Actually, substitutionary death is a moot point because Muslims believe that when the Roman soldiers came to Jesus at night in the Garden of Gethsemane, but before they laid hands on Jesus, God pulled Jesus up to heaven. Jesus was never crucified, did not shed blood, and did not die. Rather, He ascended directly to heaven.

The Love of Power vs. The Power of Love

In Islam, love is perceived to be a sign of weakness. To love is to be vulnerable. Far be it from Allah, the all-powerful, to be weak or vulnerable. What Muslims fail to recognize is that love also produces genuine confidence and hope, and it teaches the beloved to love freely and generously in return. Islam has no concept of the strength of love. It holds no belief that to be loving is a desirable character quality.

In Islam, God and man are wary of each other, whereas in Christianity, God and man are in love with each other.

This difference is of great importance because it lies at the heart of the tension Muslims feel toward Christians.

How a person relates to God is how a person relates to others. Muslims are taught—exhortations to be charitable notwithstanding—to judge, condemn, reject, avoid, ignore, and even eliminate their neighbors if those neighbors fail to measure up to their standards of faith and religious practice. Why? Because that is how they expect Allah to deal with them if they disobey his commands.

Muslims go to great extents to express their homage to the *power* of God out of their belief that God is primarily concerned with exacting tribute from an error-prone humanity. In this regard, Islam is curiously like the pre-Islamic tribal religions it so strenuously rejected. An outward show of obedience to Allah is required, far more than an inward attitude of gratitude.

The tragedy of Islam is its failure to recognize God's real concern for reestablishing a relationship of love with mankind. In an effort to give Allah honor, Islam has seriously underestimated the real power of God. Muslims simply are unable to comprehend the tremendous power of divine love that chose to live humbly as a man among men so that all might know God.

A Different Means of Relating to God

Since Muslims reject the concept of God-become-man in Jesus, they also reject the concept of the relationship between God and man that is at the heart of Christianity. Muslims not only reject the concept that God would enter into human history for the purpose of establishing—or perhaps more accurately re-establishing— a personal relationship with mankind, but Muslims reject the very idea that God has any interest whatsoever in having a personal relationship of love and friendship with man.

Christians affirm this as the meaning of Jesus' life, death, and resurrection. Jesus said to His disciples, "I no longer call you servants. . . . . Instead I have called you friends" (John 15:15) The Christian Gospel emphasizes God's offer of intimate friendship with mankind—the possibility of loving communion with God.

Islam, in sharp contrast, regards divinity and humanity as being totally exclusive entities. Muslims believe God could not have entered into human life and remained "God." Therefore, the relationship with God enjoyed by Christians is deemed impossible. Fellowship with God—which is the religious experience of the Christian—is unimaginable to Muslims. In fact, they consider the Christian assertion that man was created in God's own image to be blasphemous. (This, of course, dismisses the creation story of Genesis!)

Muslims regard the creation as an act of Allah's absolute power, and an expression of his might as lord reigning over all worlds and kingdoms. God's eternal power is clearly demonstrated in the Creation, as the Koran states:

> See they not the clouds, how they are created? And the heaven, how it is raised high and the mountains, how they are fixed and the earth, how it is spread out? (88:17–20)

Man's role, according to Islam, is as a "servant" to a "master," God. God decrees all that happens, and man has no real choice but to submit to the divine will. Allah's power, of itself, qualifies him to act as arbitrarily as he pleases. According to the Koran, "He leads and misleads whom he will." (74:34)

This concept of God "misleading" man, of course, is totally opposite to both the Jewish and Christian concepts of Jehovah. God does not misguide or mislead—He *cannot* do so because He is entirely righteous.

The Koran also states that human beings have very little choice in determining the purpose of their lives:

> Man does not enter the world or leave it as he desires. He is a creature; and the Creator, who has brought him into existence and bestowed upon him higher and more excellent faculties than upon other animals, has also assigned an object to his existence. (15:29)

Some of this may sound similar to the Bible, but in the Koran the image of the sovereign God is not tempered by a loving, compassionate nature. The Koran stresses the concept that by God's design humans should devote all their faculties to the *practice of religion*, not the *pursuit of relationship*.

Therefore stand firm in your devotion to the true faith, which Allah himself has made and for which he has made men. (30:30)

The Koran relates that God created man from the "crackling clay of black mud" and then breathed into him the breath of life:

He formed and fashioned the body of Adam from the dry clay and then he breathed into the body of his own spirit; and man, an embodied soul, came into being. (15:28–29)

On the surface, this would seem to parallel the biblical account of creation. The idea that is stressed, however, is that this makes man God's viceroy, His servant to carry out His will on the earth. There is no hint at all that this bond of "breath" signifies a spiritual relationship between God and mankind.

The Koran does not attach particular significance to the story of man's fall from communion with God—that is, the story of Adam and Eve and their sin in the Garden of Eden. There are two reasons for this: Muslims do not believe in man's original communion with God as the purpose for which man was created, and they do not believe in original sin.

The Koran's view of man's nature can be summed up this way: Man was created good—in fact, man's nature is superior to the angelic hosts, who were commanded to bow down before mankind at his creation. But being mortal, man is inconstant when tested with evil. He fell through the temptation of Satan, and he lost paradise, but he is not radically estranged from God. Man is prone to sin, but his basic nature is not sinful.

In sharp contrast, Christians believe that at the Fall something radical happened to man's nature. Man became totally sinful, alienated from God, and incapable of reconciliation with God solely through the instigation of human effort or exertion of human will. Christians also believe that the whole purpose of existence is to live in relationship with a loving God—the relationship for which we were originally created but which sin destroyed. Therefore salvation is necessary, and the redemption

Jesus Christ brought about by His death on the cross is both the restoration and the fulfillment of our reason for being.

Christians believe that man was initially created in God's image and had fellowship with God . . . that man became sinful by nature and lost fellowship with God through the initial sin committed by Adam and Eve . . . and that Jesus Christ came to take man's sin upon Himself, suffer the consequences of sin through His death on the cross, and that in dying a substitutionary death, Jesus Christ reclaimed for man the opportunity to enter into fellowship with God and reflect God's image on this earth.

Muslims categorically reject all that is stated in this preceding paragraph. They do *not* see man as totally sinful and incapable of saving himself. Muslims see a totally different relationship between man and God—man is to serve God and obey His will. In the process, the best man can hope is that he avoids God's wrath.

A Different Concept of Death and Judgment

Muslims believe that Allah decrees everything that happens, including a person's entrance into this world and death, which ushers him into the next. Birth and death are merely two aspects of the phenomenon of life that Allah owns and controls. The Koran teaches that man's hour of death is ordained:

> When their doom comes, they are not able to delay it
> an hour, nor can they advance it. (16:61)

The irrevocable finality of death is also very clearly spelled out in the Koran. When someone begs Allah to return him to earth, the answer comes:

> By no means! It is but a word that he speaks and
> before them is a barrier, until the day they are raised.
> (23:100)

Only Allah knows exactly when the Last Judgment will come:

> They ask then about the hour when will it come to
> pass? Say: The knowledge thereof is with my Lord
> only. (7:187)

Heaven and Hell. In Islam, the hereafter is divided into heaven and hell. In heaven, believers will experience God's favor and benevolence. In hell, unbelievers will experience God's severity and wrath. Both places are described in vivid terms in the Koran. Heaven is an oasis-like paradise filled with "gardens watered by running streams," rivers of milk, wine, clarified honey, and shade trees bearing all kinds of fruits.

In hell, people will be made to drink boiling water, molten metal, and decaying filth. The Koran says, "Then as for those who are unhappy, they will be in the fire; for them there will be sighing and groaning." (11:106) Hell has seven divisions, each with its particular purpose and terrors. There is a Muslim purgatory, a special division of hell for Christians, a division for Jews, and a bottomless pit for hypocrites. Many of these details are at odds with the teachings of the Bible.

The Day of Judgment. The importance of the Day of Judgment in Islam is second only to the importance of Allah himself. Muslims accept the reality of this Day of Judgment to the same degree they accept the reality that Allah exists. Some of the most striking language in the Koran is used to describe "the event which will overwhelm mankind"—this is a Day when earth and human society will be destroyed, the dead will be resurrected, and every soul will stand before God to be judged and assigned to dwell for eternity in heaven or hell. The Koran says:

> We molded man into a most noble image and in the end we shall reduce him to the lowest of the low, except the believers who do good works, for theirs shall be a boundless recompense. What, then can after this make you deny the Last Judgment? Is Allah not the best of judges? (95:4–8)

Allah is not only the benevolent Creator who generously lavishes on mankind all earthly blessings, but also the vengeful Judge who, having demanded absolute submission to his absolute divine will, mercilessly imposes inevitable and terrible punishment on those who spurn him and transgress his laws. This belief stands in stark contrast to Christianity's loving God, who, even as He judges in righteousness, is "patient with you, not wanting anyone to perish." (2 Pet. 3:9)

As for the last Judgment itself, the clearest and most concise description of the Muslim's view is found in L. Bevan Jones' book, *The People of the Mosque* (Calcutta: Associated Press, YMCA, 1932). Bevan summarizes that the Last Day will not come until there is no one found who calls on God. Then the "sounding of the trumpet" will signal the arrival of the Day of Judgment. The Last Day and subsequent Judgment unfold in a precise sequence:

1. At the first blast of the trumpet, everyone in heaven and earth will die except those whom God saves.

2. At the second trumpet blast, the dead are resurrected.

3. After the resurrection, a period of forty years occurs. During this time people will wander about the earth naked, confused, and sorrowful. They must await "the descent of the books" that have been kept by the recording angels. Each book will be given to its owner, delivered into the right hand of those who are good and into the left hand of those who are wicked.

4. The "scales" weigh each one's good and bad deeds, and the fate of each individual is determined. Good deeds are heavy; bad deeds are lighter in weight. Prophets and angels are exempt from this trial, and according to some authorities, so are believers.

5. The preceding tests concludes, everyone will be required to cross "the bridge," a very narrow road "sharper than the edge of a sword, finer than a hair, suspended over hell." (36:66) Those who are to be saved will pass over it quickly, but those who are condemned will fall into hell and remain there forever.

A popular belief among Muslims is that Jesus will return as the Last Day approaches, declare Himself to be a Muslim, and will call the entire world to Islam. Then He will die a normal death.

In Islam, the promise of eternal life is always linked to good works—and to a predominance of good works over bad deeds. The Koran records twenty-four times that Allah does not love sinners (2:190 and following), but only those who fear him. (3:76) Salvation for sinners does not exist in Islam.

To be a Muslim is to believe in Allah, his messenger Muhammad, and the Last Judgment. And since Muslims believe in very precise rules of conduct, *not* to live as the Koran instructs is practically to guarantee damnation in unending torment. Thus, the underlying motivation for faith and religious practice is fear.

Where Do These Differences Lead?

As you read through these comparative differences, it should be readily obvious that

- Islam has adopted only *partial* segments of the teaching of the Bible, and especially the New Testament
- Islam and Christianity have great differences in their understanding of the nature of God, the nature of man, and the way in which God and man relate

Where do these differences lead? They lead to a distinctively different "outworking" of belief—a different prescription for living.

In Christianity, on the other hand, it is a personal relationship with God through Christ that leads to a life of required submission, exertion of will, the doing of "good works." In Islam, a person hopes to be made acceptable for God's consideration by his or her deeds.

The beliefs of Christianity lead to a life of faith, the choice to live in obedience to God's commandments, and the expression of virtuous character (fruit of the Spirit) that results in moral, ethical living. In Christianity, a person is made acceptable for fellowship with God by faith in the shed blood of Jesus Christ.

The difference is profound, and it has a direct bearing on the ultimate "expression" of literal Islam—terrorism.

A Brief Overview of Islam and Christianity

Here is a very brief overview of the concepts that are central to both Islam and Christianity:

	Islam	Christianity
1. God	Distant (unknowable) Does not reveal himself —reveals only his will Merciful (forgives at His will) Capricious (both "leads" and misleads") Vengeful (honor restored only by "getting even") Almighty (emphasis on power)	Personal (can be known) Revealed himself in Incarnation of Jesus Christ Loving Concerned for individual Just Holy Almighty (power balanced with love)
2. Christ	Prophet Total denial of incarnation	God's Son
3. Bible	Revealed by God Changed and corrupted by unfaithful Jews and Christians	Revealed by God Authoritative Word
4. Trinity	God, Mary, and Jesus (Islam's view of the Christian trinity)	Father, Son, and Holy Spirit
5. Faith	Intellectual agreement that Allah is One and Muhammad is Prophet	Recognition that man is a sinner unable to save himself but trusts in Christ's substitutionary payment for his sins
6. Sin	Shame, embarrassment Rebellion against God Dishonor to family People are inherently good Absolved by good works	Rebellion against God (primarily) and man; result is guilt Requires divine forgiveness All people are born with a sin nature, but a just God requires that the penalty be paid — Jesus paid it
7. Salvation	Provided by God at His will Faith and works prerequisite Cannot be assured	Provided by God to all who trust in Jesus Christ's atoning death on the cross; works do not lead to salvation
8. Sanctification	Emphasis on ritual and obedience to Koran External and ceremonial Keep five pillars	Emphasis on the growth of the Christian into Christ-likeness, through the work of the Holy Spirit
9. Love	Erotic and familial	Spiritual (God's love — agape; sacrificial love) Family, romantic love, friendship, and erotic love all recognized
10. Supernatural	Believe in unseen world Realm with angels on left and right (good/bad) Satan is regarded as force of hate and power Fatalistic—all is preordained by God	Believe in angels and demons as described in Bible Satan is arch enemy of God; totally evil with lesser power than God Man can overcome evil only through the power of God given to him by the Holy Spirit

Chapter Four

DIFFERENT
PRESCRIPTIONS FOR
LIVING

At its core—in belief and in genuine practice—Christianity is a faith of love, forgiveness, and new life. "Law," for the most part, is left to the politics of secular society. Denomination-related statutes are not imposed outside the denomination. Respect is given to governing authorities. A belief exists in separation of church and state. This separation of church and state provides a framework in which great tolerance can be given to the freedom to express religion and opinion; the tendency is toward democracy in some form and to some degree.

Islam, in sharp contrast, is a religion of law, submission, and punishment. The ideal world according to Islam is a world that is ordered by Islamic beliefs with *no* separation of religion and state. Since there is no separation between church and state, the ideal political leader is the religious leader. There is no tolerance given to other religions; the tendency is toward autocracy and absolute theocracy.

In a very practical way, Islam and Christianity give different "prescriptions" for living—how a person is to express his beliefs, order his schedule, and manage his possessions.

The Christian Prescription

The prescription for living of Christians can be summed up in one statement, voiced first in Judaism and then by Jesus: Love God, and love one's neighbors. (See Deut. 6:5 and Matt. 22:37–40.)

Certainly many professing Christians display unloving behavior—Christians are not immune to self-righteousness, prejudice, hatred, anger, and bitterness. But there is nothing in Christianity that condones, much less endorses, an unloving attitude or behavior. To the contrary, the true Christian constantly strives with the help of God to weed from his or her life anything that hinders the growth of God's love. For the genuine Christian, the self-giving love of God revealed in Jesus Christ is the same love the Christian is called upon to express to others. Jesus' clear command to His followers was, "Love each other as I have loved you." (John 15:12)

Christians always have fallen short of living up to Christ's example. The history of Christianity is filled with spectacular examples of such failure: the Crusades, the Spanish Inquisition of the Middle Ages, and the vicious extremism of contemporary Northern Ireland. Genuine Christians regard these incidents in history with shame and tend to blame them on misguided zeal. Christians acknowledge and understand human weakness, and the persistent tendency in the human heart to turn against one's neighbor, but it also considers these acts of hatred to be rooted in ignorance and evil perversions of the love of Christ. The overriding belief of orthodox Christians through the ages has been that genuine Christians are known by their love. John wrote eloquently about this in his letters:

- "This is the message you heard from the beginning: We should love one another. Do not be like Cain, who belonged to the evil one and murdered his brother." (1 John 3:11)

- "Anyone who hates his brother is a murderer, and you know that no murderer has eternal life in him." (1 John 3:15)

- "This is how we know what love is: Jesus Christ laid down his life for us. And we ought to lay down our lives for our brothers . . . . Dear children, let us not love with words or tongue but with actions and in truth." (1 John 3:16, 18)

- "This is his command: to believe in the name of his Son, Jesus Christ, and to love one another as he commanded us." (1 John 3:23)

The message of God's love and a call to love one another rings loud and clear throughout the Gospels. Jesus said, "For God so loved the world that he gave his one and only Son, that whoever believes in him shall not perish but have eternal life. For God did not send his Son into the world to condemn the world, but to save the world through him." (John 3:16–17)

Jesus also said, "Love your enemies, do good to those who hate you, bless those who curse you, pray for those who mistreat you . . . . Love your enemies, do good to them, and lend to them without expecting to get anything back. Then your reward will be great, and you will be sons of the Most High, because he is kind to the ungrateful and wicked. Be merciful, just as your Father is merciful." (Luke 6:27–28, 35–36)

Jesus said, "Do not judge, and you will not be judged. Do not condemn, and you will not be condemned. Forgive, and you will be forgiven." (Luke 6:37)

Forgiveness. Christianity calls upon the faithful to confess their faults to one another, to forgive freely, and to seek to make amends when wrongs have been committed.

Muslims and others frequently point toward the Crusades and the Inquisition as the two giant black eyes of Christianity in history.

After taking Jerusalem in 1099, the Crusaders slaughtered innocent men, women, and children—Muslims, Jews, and even other Christians. Islamic historians have exaggerated the death toll, but there can be no justification for what the Crusaders did in the name of Christ. Most Christians today do not make excuses for the Crusaders. They are appalled at what happened.

On the one thousandth anniversary of the fall of Jerusalem, Pope John Paul II apologized for the actions of the Crusaders and called the events in Jerusalem and others like it "departures" from the Spirit of Christ and His Gospel.

There isn't likely to be a similar apology for the actions of Muslim armies against Christians and Jews. Islam's spread was the product of military conquest, not peaceable conversions, and for the most part, the degree of massacre, enslavement, and other brutality exceeded anything done by the Christians from Europe.

The reason that Christianity can own up to its failures lies in the fact that the Gospel of Jesus challenges believers to love their neighbors *and* their enemies. There is no equivalent for this in Islam. The Koran commands Muslims to wage war on the unbeliever and to annihilate him. In contrast, Christians are to win their enemies to Christ by acts of compassion and charity.

The Prescription of Islam

In sharp contrast to Christianity, Islam is a religion of law, blind submission, and punishment. In strict Islamic society, submitting to the ruler is equal with submitting to Allah.

Islam doesn't simply require "belief" in Allah, the Koran, Muhammad as the prophet, and the Day of Judgment. It requires *submission* to Allah. A tribe in seventh century Arabia acknowledged to Muhammad their faith in Allah, saying, "We believe in Allah!" Muhammad supposedly responded, "You have not believed until you say, 'We have submitted ourselves!'" (Sura 49:14)

As stated previously, the first confession of the Koran is "there is no God except Allah" and "Muhammad is his prophet." In light of history, a more accurate interpretation would be: "There is no God who is allowed to be worshiped except Allah, and every man *must* follow Muhammad and his teachings."

The Five Pillars. The five pillars of Islam summarize the Muslim's fundamental religious duties and beliefs:

1. CONFESSION (*shahada*). This means reciting the statement, "There is no God but Allah. Muhammad is the Prophet of God."

2. PRAYER. Formal prayers are to be recited five times a day: before sunrise, after midday, at mid-afternoon, shortly after sunset, and in the fullness of night. Prayer involves bowing in the direction of the city of Mecca.

3. PAYING THE ALMS TAX (*zakat*). The legal zakat or "purification" tax is levied on property. All Muslims for the benefit of the poor, which may include one's own family members, the needy, and at times, the poor stranger who is traveling through an area, pay it. The amount of the zakat is fixed—usually about two

and a half percent of one's wealth. In some circumstances, the amount is more.

4. FASTING AND PRAYERS AT RAMADAN. This is generally limited to the holy month of Ramadan, the month in which Muslims believe the first verses of the Koran were revealed to Muhammad in 610 A.D.

   Between sunrise and sunset, adult Muslims do not smoke, eat, drink, or engage in sexual intercourse. They are encouraged to read the Koran from beginning to end during the month. They may eat and drink between sunset and sunrise. Ramadan is both the name of the ninth month on the Islamic calendar (a lunar calendar), and the name of the period of religious observance marked by fasting. The three days that follow Ramadan are a feasting period, a time for alms-giving and exchange of gifts.

5. PILGRIMAGE. Every Muslim of sound body, sane, and able to afford the journey is expected to make a pilgrimage, called *Hajj*, to Mecca at least once in his or her lifetime. Those who make the pilgrimage may add "al-Hajj" to their names.

These are regarded as the *minimal* obligations of every good Muslim. They alone, however, are not adequate to ensure that one is living a virtuous life . . . rather, they are the *prerequisites* of virtue.

In addition to the five pillars, Muslims are expected to "commend good and reprimand evil" and they are forbidden to gamble, charge interest on loans made to fellow Muslims, and consume alcohol or pork.

Different Meaning in Keeping the Five Pillars. All Muslims are strictly commanded to keep the Five Pillars. What these pillars mean to Muslims, however, varies.

Orthodox Muslims—sometimes called believers in "high Islam" are those who tend to be trained in the Koran, more educated, and of higher cultural status. Hundreds of millions of Muslims, however, are considered to be "low" Muslims—less formal in their understanding, less educated in the Koran, more "superstitious," and more likely to interpret Islam according to their cultural "folklore" and customs. The differences play out in these very basic ways:

	"High Islam"	"Low" Islam
Confession	Proves one is true Muslim	Words are used to drive away evil
Prayer Ritual	Bodily washing results in purification	Demonic pollution is removed
Legal Alms	Responsibility to fellow Muslims	Precaution against evil eye
Fasting	Sign of commitment to Islam	Rituals that deal with evil and sickness
Pilgrimage	Visit to epicenter of faith	Rituals deal with devil and sickness

By the way, the Sufis are the mystics of Islam. Sufis seek to be completely reliant upon God (*tawakkul*) and to keep God in perpetual remembrance (*dhikr*). The Sufi movement has developed inside the lines of orthodox Islamic practice, but many in Islam regard them as heretical because they seek direct contact with God.

Emphasis on Behavior. As you may have concluded, the main emphasis in Islam is on *external behavior*, not the inward transformation of a person's heart, mind, and will. Islam is a religion of externals—overt acts that one must do to put himself or herself in the ballpark for receiving God's favor.

There is nothing in Islam that states God loves a man or woman simply for who that person is as His creation. Rather, Islam states that God may or may not show favor to men and women who obey His commands—for a person even to be considered for favor, the five pillars must be kept.

Christians may be tempted to regard all this as "salvation by works." Salvation, however, is not a concept Islam accepts. Remember, according to Islam, man doesn't have a sinful nature and therefore, man's nature does not need to be transformed.

A thoughtful Muslim must experience a certain amount of anxiety at all times—after all, it is never possible to be *assured* that one's actions have earned acquittal before the eternal Judge. A Muslim must be vigilant constantly, exercising alertness mixed with fear at every moment of every day, just to be *considered* for *possible* favor. Just as sin is not a part of man's essential nature, neither is forgiveness essential to Allah's nature. Allah is not bound by his own nature to forgive man—it is something he chooses to do somewhat consistently, but with no guarantee that he will do so in every instance.

There is, however, not doubt as to what Allah expects of a person if a person is to have *any hope* of being admitted to paradise in the next life. Even the most devout or pious Muslim, cannot be assured of winning Allah's favor and of entering paradise. Muslims pray to Allah with a certain amount of cajoling and begging. They are asked to bow before a deity unwilling to give any assurance that the sinner is forgiven.

The end result is that insecurity and fear of God—a fear bordering on terror—are integral to Islam. These beliefs foster an even greater defensiveness on the part of Muslims who encounter non-Muslims. After all, if a Muslim cannot know with certainty that he is forgiven . . . how can he readily forgive others? In addition, these beliefs foster greater aggressiveness in dealing with non-Muslims. After all, if a Muslim sees Allah as judgmental and unyielding in demanding subjection to his will, it stands to reason that Muslims in turn should be judgmental and unyielding in demanding subjection.

What About Those Who Don't Believe

Christianity regards those who do not believe in Christ as being "unconverted." The unconverted are to be told the Gospel of Jesus Christ and given an opportunity to *accept* Him as their Savior—this is the essence of Christian evangelism. The act of acceptance is an act of free will.

Islam considers those who do not adhere to Islam to be "infidels." They are to be subjected to the will of Allah. Subjection does not require free will on the part of the person being subjected!

This is a critical distinction to recognize. It lies at the heart of the terrorism we have experienced and are likely to continue to experience at the hands of Muslim zealots.

Many Westerners have asked me through the years, "Why are Muslims so fanatical about their religion?" A secondary question is this: "Why is it that the more devout one becomes to Islam, the more intolerant that person becomes to other religions?"

From the viewpoint of Islam, Muslims believe they alone have been given "the final revelation" of God in the Koran. I say final because most Muslims respect the Torah (the five books of Moses) and the *Injeil* (their version of the Gospel). But from the commands of their sacred book, the *Koran*, they believe they are called to *enforce* God's will. The Koran challenges all Islamic followers—moderate or zealot, young or old, religious or secular—to convert or conquer unbelievers. Note again the two options: convert or conquer. To the Muslim idealist, there is no room for moderation. The economic wealth and political power of Islamic leaders in many nations allows this uncompromising, harsh, and intolerant imperative to manifest itself on a grand scale.

We must never lose sight of the ultimate goal of Islam—the submission of all people to Islamic control, which is, in the words of the Koran, the fulfillment of God's will for all people.

In the end, the political and economic and militaristic—yes, even terrorist—actions of Khomeini, Saddam Hussein, the decisions of the royal family in Saudi Arabia, the aggressive statements from Libyan strongman Moammar Khadafy and other Islamic leaders before him (including Egypt's Nasser), and the strident words from Osama bin Laden and the Al Qaeda leadership are all rooted in this concept of "enforcement" of Allah's will upon infidels. Indeed, the occupation of Lebanon by Syria, the Palestinian cause in Israel, and the intolerance for Christianity in all Muslim-dominated nations—including Indonesia, Sudan, and others—must be understood in terms of Islam's goal: the subjugation of all people to Islamic beliefs and Islamic law.

Islamic Law and Islamic Thought

Islamic law is at the core of Islamic thought. There are various interpretations for how Islamic laws are to be *implemented*, but there is little disagreement about the core idea: Non-Muslims do not belong to the House of Islam (Dar al-Islam), and therefore, they belong to the House of War (Dar al-Harb). In simple language, if you aren't with us, you are against us. Infidels—those who do not believe in Islam—are to be humiliated, denied due process of law, and ultimately, coerced into conversion or killed. The Koran says very forthrightly:

Fight against such as those who have been given the Scripture as believe not in Allah nor the Last Day. (9:29) (The word "scripture" in this verse refers to the Koran, not the Bible.)

No genuine Christian reformer could or would pursue such a philosophy and remain true to the whole of Christian doctrine. But to follow such a strategy is precisely what makes a Muslim true to Muslim doctrine. Using this verse as justification, Muslim zealots consider moderate Muslims—those who claim to be Muslims but do not follow the letter of the law—to be infidels, also, equally deserving the same treatment as non-Muslims.

There are only three alternatives for dealing with non-Muslims under Islamic law:

- they must be converted
- they must be subjugated or humiliated
- they must be eliminated (except women, children, and slaves)

Islamic law distinguishes between types of non-Muslims. Christians and Jews are in different categories than other non-Muslims.

Some Muslim states permit an "infidel" to enter a formal agreement or treaty that spares the unbeliever's life and property. In those cases, the non-Muslim becomes classified as *dhimmi* and is *subjugated* in various ways. A *dhimmi* must wear identifiable clothing and live in a clearly marked house. He must not ride a horse or bear arms. He must always yield the right-of-way to Muslims. A *dhimmi* cannot be a witness in a legal court except in matters relating to other *dhimmis*. He cannot be the guardian of a Muslim child, owner of a Muslim slave, or a judge in a Muslim court. (A.S. Tritton, *The Caliphs and Their non-Muslim Subjects* [London: Frank Cass and Company, 1970])

The concept of *dhimmi* is of great significance because Islamic fundamentalists—those who interpret the Koran and Islamic law in the narrowest, most literal sense— often take minor concepts and establish major policies that affect Islamic society, political systems, and economic practice. The *dhimmi* mentality smolders just beneath the fire of many relationships between Muslims and non-Muslims.

Three categories of *dhimmi* are identified in Islam: Hudna, Musta'min, and Zimmi.

Hudna ("truce") are those who sign a peace treaty with Muslims after being defeated in war. They may continue to reside on their own land, yet are subject to the laws of Islam.

Musta'min ("protected ones") are those who come to an Islamic nation as messengers, merchants, visitors, or students wanting to learn about Islam. They are obliged to pay *Jizya* (tribute, a "protection tax") and must not engage in war against Muslims. If they do not accept Islam, they are allowed to return safely to their own country, but once in their homeland, they are treated as those belonging to the Household of War.

Zimmis (literally "those in custody") are non-Muslims who live in Muslim countries and agree to pay the Jizya in exchange for protection and safety, and agree to be subject to Islamic law. The imposition of the protection tax is intended to be an act of humiliation and subjugation.

Zimmis are not allowed to build new churches, temples, or synagogues. They may renovate "old churches," which are considered to be those in existence prior to Islamic conquest. No church, temple, or synagogue may be built in Saudi Arabia (or the entire Arab Peninsula)—that land is considered "sacred" since it was the land of Muhammad.

Zimmis are not allowed to pray or read their sacred books out loud at home or in churches, in case Muslims hear their prayers.

Zimmis are not allowed to print their religious books or sell them in public places and markets. They are not allowed to install the cross on their houses or churches. They are not allowed to broadcast or display ceremonial religious rituals on radio or television, or to use any form of media to publish any picture related to their religious ceremonies. They are not allowed to congregate in the streets during their religious festivals or to join the army (unless there is an indispensable need for them, in which case they may be conscripted for service but not hold leadership positions).

Muslims are not allowed to emulate the Zimmis in their dress or behavior, to attend Zimmi festivals or support them in any way. They are not to lease their houses or sell land for the construction of a church, temple, liquor store, or anything that may benefit the Zimmi's faith. They may not work for Zimmis in any job that might promote their faith (such as constructing a church), make any financial gift to a church or temple, or address Zimmis with any title such as "my master" or "my lord."

Muslims may console Zimmis in an illness or in the loss of a loved one. They may escort a funeral to the cemetery, but they are to walk in front of the coffin, not behind it, and they must depart before the deceased is buried. Muslims may congratulate Zimmis for a wedding, birth of a child, return from a long trip, or recovery from illness. They are not, however, to utter any word that may suggest approval of the Zimmis' faith, such as "May Allah exalt you," "May Allah honor you," or "May Allah give your religion victory."

What does all this mean to us in the West? *Dhimmi*—and in particular, *Zimmi*, is the classification given to Christians in most Muslim countries. These are the restrictions under which Christians must live and work. In fact, this is how the Saudi government treated our soldiers when they went to defend them during the Gulf War.

If you understand *how* Christians are required to live in Islamic nations, you will have a better understanding about how to pray for your brothers and sisters in Christ who are living in those nations!

Most non-Muslims are not regarded as citizens by any Islamic state, even if they are original natives of the land. That is why Muslin extremists in countries such as Egypt, Syria, Lebanon, and even Iraq, where Christians are somewhat tolerated, want to topple these regimes because they do not consider these nations to be *Islamic* states.

We in the West also need to recognize clearly that when a nation becomes "Islamic" by law—declaring itself to be an Islamic State—the native people of that land who are of any religion other than Islam suddenly become second-class citizens.

Let me briefly give you the example of Egypt.

Islam first came to Egypt in the middle 600s A.D. The largest group to withstand the onslaught of Islam was the Coptic Church. Founded in 42 A.D. by Mark, the author of the second Gospel, the Coptic Church had six hundred years to become established before the Muslims overran Egypt. The cost of refusing to convert to Islam was very often paid in terms of human life. Those who were not martyred were taxed heavily.

Today in Egypt, the Copts have retained much of their original heritage. About seven million Egyptians are Coptic Christians—

they make up between ten and fifteen percent of the Egyptian population.

Life has not ceased to be difficult for the Copts. Radical Islamic organizations continue to pressure the government to return to the concept of *dhimmi*, which would make Copts second-class citizens. The Muslim Brotherhood specifically targets Egyptian Copts for violence. Property is destroyed; people are beaten, maimed, and killed. In periodic waves, Christian shops, restaurants, homes, as well as at least one cathedral and a number of Protestant churches have been destroyed.

Westerners who are steeped in the tradition of separation of church and state have genuine difficulty with these ideas. For their part, Muslims have genuine difficulty *accepting* separation of church and state. They see the two as connected, not only in their own culture but in other cultures. Muslims overseas cannot differentiate between the Western way of life and the Judeo-Christian ethical system. They assume that all Americans are Jews or Christians since our values are rooted in the Judeo-Christian ethical system. They see their fellow Muslims living in America as "strangers in a strange land"—Muslims are expected, whenever possible, to keep themselves separate from the culture as a whole. They are expected to give their greater allegiance to Islam, not the state.

What About Those Who Oppose Islam?

Those who oppose Islam—or who are perceived to be standing in the way of the advancement of Islam—are considered infidels of the highest order. They not only *may* be killed in the process of subjugation, but they *deserve* to be killed. In some sectors of Islam, they *should* be killed as a matter of obedience to Allah.

It is the subjugation of non-Islamic people, and particularly those who oppose Islam, that is at the heart of *jihad*. Jihad is the *first word* learned in the reading primers of Palestinian schools—it is the *first word* uttered in many assaults on Western people and property . . . it is the *first word* on the lips of those who sponsor or support terrorism. The meaning of this term is where we turn next.

Chapter Five

JIHAD

The term *jihad*, often used to communicate the concept of "holy war," literally means *struggle.*

Three types of *jihad* are generally recognized by Muslim, scholars: the *jihad* of one's self—a matter of self-discipline and the fight against evil in one's own mind and heart; the *jihad* of Satan, which Christians would call spiritual warfare; and the *jihad* of infidels and hypocrites—the fight against all who reject or stand in the way of the advancement of Islam. Some have tried to state that these three facets are "stages," but in reality, the three co-exist in Islam when Islam is viewed as a whole.

Forsaking *jihad* is the reason many Muslims are perceived to suffer today. Those who hold this opinion often site this statement in the Koran:

> O ye who believe! What aileth you that when it is said unto you: Go forth in the way of Allah, ye are bowed down to the ground with heaviness. Take ye pleasure in the life of the world rather than in the Hereafter? The comfort of the life of the world is but little in comparison with that in the Hereafter. If ye go not forth He will afflict

you with a painful doom, and will choose instead of you a folk other than you. Ye cannot harm Him at all. Allah is Able to do all things. (9:38–39)

Not every Muslim agrees that *jihad* requires spilling the blood of infidels—and there are those who insist that the "struggle" refers only to an individual's own personal struggle against evil. Nevertheless, the *struggle* for the victory of Islam is a factor in the life of every faithful Muslim. Even those who see *jihad* as a personal religious term must acknowledge that through the centuries and even today, Muslims as a whole regard *jihad* as the struggle for the teachings of Islam to gain preeminence over all other religious teachings.

Al-Banna explained the importance of *jihad* this way:

> How wise was the man who said, "force is the surest way of implementing the right and how beautiful it is that force and right should march side by side." This striving to broadcast the Islamic mission, quite apart from preserving the hallowed concepts of Islam, is another religious duty imposed by God on the Muslims, just as he imposed fasting, prayer, pilgrimage, alms, and the doing of good and abandonment of evil, upon them. He imposes it upon them and delegated them to do it. He did not excuse anyone possessing strength and capacity from performing it. (Hasan Al-Banna, "To What Do We Summon Mankind?" *Five Tracts of Hasan Al-Banna*, trans. Charles Wendell [Berkeley: University of California Press, 1978], 80)

Jihad, according to Islamic law, is to be waged until the Day of Judgment—or forever. There may be times when Muslim armies appear to be defeated, but even legal armistices can be broken when they are perceived (by Muslims) to be in the best interests of Islam. Islam allows for *no possible permanent peaceful equality with infidels*. Superiority is such a vital factor in Islamic thought that domination is the only worthy expression of Islam's greatness.

It is not strange, therefore, to read in the Koran that Allah exhorts Muslims *not* to make friends with Jews or Christians:

> Oh ye who believe! Take not the Jews and Christians for friends. They are friends one to another. He among you who taketh them for friends is one of them. (5:51)

Elsewhere, the Koran states:

> Believers, do not make friends with anyone other than your own people. They desire nothing but ruin. Their hatred is clear from what they say, but more violent is the hatred that their breasts conceal. (3:118)

Extremists, of course, take quotes such as these as proof that they are to *enforce* an intolerant attitude toward non-Muslims. The result are laws and rules that prohibit interaction between Muslims and those who are not of their own "brotherhood."

Extremists also routinely exhort the "faithful" to begin a holy war against Jews, Christians, and other non-Muslims.

Those who are not extremists sometimes state that they believe these texts were only for certain historical periods, and that they are not binding upon Muslims today. Those voices tend to be few, however, and they do not echo the sentiments of the vast majority of Muslims around the world.

Islamic "superiority" has its apex in the Koran, Surah5: 33. In this statement, Muslims are commanded to *fight* non-Muslims and anyone who rejects Allah and his apostle (Muhammad). How are they to deal with the enemies of Islam? By crucifying them, cutting off their hands and feet on alternate sides, or banishing them from the country.

Many scoff today when *jihad* is declared by a fairly small group of extremists in a small nation about which little is known. The imperative to subjugate non-Muslims, however, runs deep among Muslims around the world—not just in the hills and caves of Afghanistan or remote enclaves in third-world nations. *Jihad* is an essential ingredient of the love of Islamic philosophy—it is the nail on which all attempts to justify and demand the use of extreme power to accomplish Islamic purposes are hung.

Muslims have been left to define for themselves the "means" of waging *jihad* against infidels. They are generally advised to use whatever means of victory will result in minimum loss of life to the Muslims fighting. That certainly was the approach to what occurred September 11, 2001—twenty or fewer Muslims took out more than 3,000 "Westerners" and a great deal of property. From the Islamic point of view, this was a successful battle.

No Mercy from Islamic Fundamentalists

There is no mercy in the Koran or in Islam as a whole for those who oppose the *advancement* of Islam. While passages of the Koran decry the murder of innocents and urge mercy and tolerance toward "life" in general, there is no mercy extended to those who stand in the path of Islam's evangelistic efforts.

The Koran states:

- When the sacred months are past, kill those who join other gods wherever you find them, and seize them, beleaguer them, and lie in wait for them with every kind of ambush; but if they convert and observe prayer and pay the obligatory alms, let them go their way. (Sura 9:5)

- strive hard against the unbelievers and the hypocrites, and be firm against them. Their abode is Hell, an evil refuge indeed. (Sura 9:73)

The terms "militant" and "fundamentalist" have come to mean the same thing in certain circles—whether the terms are applied to Muslims, Christians, or Jews. Fundamentalists are those perceived to withdraw from mainstream society to form sacred enclaves of pure faith, and in that sanctuary, the faithful study their own doctrine, create a counter-culture, and then react—often with a political, military, or social offensive— against those whom they believe are in error before God and a threat to the "true" path they themselves espouse.

In its pure sense, fundamentalist means to hold the "fundamentals" of a faith very close to the heart, and to attempt to live out the fundamentals of that faith in a practical way.

Not all fundamentalists are militant. In fact, the vast majority of those who believe strongly in the Bible's commandments— whether Jew or Christian—are not militaristic, separatist, counter-cultural, or on the offensive. That simply is not the case in Islam. Those who believe strongly in the fundamentals of Islam are nearly always militaristic.

Norman Geisler, author of *Answering Islam,* co-written by Abdul Saleeb, (Baker Book House, 1994), has said, "What Islam engages in is consistent with the teachings of the Qur'an and Muhammad while what some Christians did in the Crusades is contrary to the teachings of the Bible and Jesus Christ." He has also said, "Violence is the logical outworking of Islam and the illogical outworking of Christianity." ("Doug Potter, "Southern Evangelical Seminary Dives into Islam" [*Charlotte World* January 2002])

While the means of expressing and enforcing *jihad* is discussed in Islamic circles, the ultimate goal of *jihad* is not debated—non-Muslims are to be put into submission to Allah. We should also recognize that a power struggle between radical Muslims and "moderate" Muslims is inevitable—the two forces have never, do not, and cannot peacefully coexist. The goal of radical Muslims is the domination of the world and absolute adherence to the strictest interpretation of Islamic law. Moderates, in the eyes of the radicals, are only one step removed from non-Muslims when it comes to being a foe that stands in the way of Islam's supremacy and advancement.

Around the world, it has always been the more zealous, rigid, radical voices that have been heard the loudest, heeded with the most passion, and heralded as the most faithful. It is the radical voice that spews hate and inspires terrorism.

Washing Blood with Blood

A well-known Muslim saying states, "One must wash blood with blood." Islamic terrorists take that saying literally.

Consider these statements from well-known Islamic leaders:

- Just one week after the United States Marine battalion headquarters in Lebanon were bombed, Sheikh Muhammad Yazbeck said, "Let America, Israel, and the world know that we have a lust for martyrdom and our motto is being translated into reality." (Robin Wright, *Sacred Rage: The Wrath of Militant Islam* [New York: Simon and Schuster, 1985], 99)

- Hussein Musawi, leader of the Islamic Amal movement has said: "This path is the path of blood, the path of martyrdom. For us death is easier than smoking a cigarette if it comes while fighting for the cause of God and while defending the oppressed." (Wright, *Sacred Rage*, 83–84)

- the founder of the Muslim Brotherhood of Egypt, Hasan Al-Banna, said this to his followers:

  You are not a benevolent organization, nor a political party, nor a local association with limited aims. Rather, you are a new spirit making its way into the heart of this nation, and reviving it through the Koran; a new light dawning and scattering the darkness of materialism through the knowledge of God; a resounding voice rising and echoing the message of the Apostle. (Hasan Al-Banna, "Between Yesterday and Today," *Five Tracts of Hasan Al-Banna, Trans. Charles Wendell [Berkeley: University of California Press], 36)*

- Shukri Ahmed Mustafa, a leader of the Muslim Brotherhood offshoot group accused in the killing of the former Egyptian Minister of Trusts and Bequests, said his movement's philosophy was based on "sacred hatred" of Islamic nations he believes have departed from the true faith. Mustafa told a reporter before he was hanged in 1978, "Spilling the blood of heretics is the sacred duty of all Muslims." Mustafa saw the minister's assassination as part of a pattern of assassinations, including the assassination of Anwar Sadat, as a means of prodding the masses into Islamic revolution. The goal was to spur Egypt to becoming the "Islamic Republic of Egypt" and from there, to the world becoming Islamic.

Let me add this almost parenthetically: The Islamic Jihad organization of Egypt did not come to the world's attention until Sadat was killed, just as Al Qaeda did not become a household word prior to September 11, 2001. Both organizations, however, existed long before the tragic events that catapulted them to notoriety. Those who have followed the history of these groups very closely know that the Islamic Jihad has merged with other groups to become Al Qaeda (the foundation). The Muslim Brotherhood, which fathered all of these groups, was founded in

1928, and had a surge of popularity in the 1950s before President Gamal Abdel Nasser imprisoned its leaders. Many members of the group were placed in concentration camps or hanged because of assassination attempts on Nasser. Ironically, it was Sadat who released the Muslim Brotherhood leaders from prison after he came to power in 1970, in order to use them to fight Nasser's leftist "centers of power."

We should be under no illusion that simply by rounding up a couple of hundred—even several thousand— Al Qaeda leaders around the world, we will bring an end to Muslim-fueled terrorism. That simply has not been, is not now, and will never be the case. Islamic purists see all other religions as heretical or hopelessly corrupt. They tolerate no view other than their own. They believe it is Allah's will for all societies to come under the Islamic flag and Islamic law and religion. They believe only a doctrinally pure, incorrupt Islamic nation can please Allah and anything else must be redeemed or destroyed. That *spirit* of Islam will not die with the death of Al Qaeda leaders or conspirators. It is endemic to the religion.

The Bloody Example of Khomeini's Iran

After he assumed power in Iran, Khomeini came down hard on everything that was not according to his interpretation of Islamic law and tradition. Iran suffered a torrent of executions, bomb explosions, murders, and other atrocities.

Khomeini, however, did not only target officials of the Shah's regime. He also targeted members of the Mojahedin, an Islamic fundamentalist organization that had a leftist ideology and that had been involved in a very active guerrilla movement against the former Shah. Within months, twenty-five hundred Mojahedin followers had been arrested and executed by hanging and firing squads.

The Mojahedin countered with its own brand of terror, blowing hundreds of Khomeini officials to pieces by merciless suicide attacks. The majority of the suicide assassins were young, aged fifteen to twenty-five. The Mojahedin declaration of June 20, 1981 (issued in the aftermath of the first wave of Khomeini's executions), said in part:

> Khordad 30th (June 20,1981) is our Ashura. On that day we had to stand up and resist Khomeini's blood-

thirsty and reactionary regime, even if it meant sacrificing our lives and the whole of our organization. We
had to take this road to Karbala to keep alive our
tawhidi ideology, follow the example set by Imam
Hussein, fulfill our historic mission to the Iranian people, and fight the most bloodthirsty, most reactionary,
and most savage regime in world history. (Ervand
Abrahamian, *The Iranian Mojahedin* [New Haven, CT:
Yale University Press, 1989], 220)

Khomeini voiced almost the same blood-thirsty sentiment:

Our nation is no longer ready to submit to humiliation
and abjection; it prefers a bloody death to a life of
shame. We are ready to be killed, and we have made a
covenant with God to follow the path of our leader,
the Lord of Martyrs. (Ayatollah Khomeini, *Islam and
Revolution: Writings and Declarations of Imam Khomeini,*
trans. Hamid Algar [Berkeley, CA: Mizan Press, 1981],
305)

The bloodshed between the Islamic government of Khomeini
and the Mojahedin continued for four years and in all, more
than 12,250 political dissidents died, three-quarters of them
Mojahedin members or sympathizers.

The horror of these killings went largely unreported in the
West—many in the West viewed this bloodshed as something of
a civil war in Iran. These killings are brought up here to point out
that suicide bombings are not limited to the Palestinians in
Israel. Much of what the Palestinians learned they learned from
the Khomeini-Mojahedin conflict as far back as 1981.

The killings by Khomeini's associates were justified in this
way: Shiites were taking revenge on the 680 A.D. murder of
Hussein (a descendant of the prophet Muhammad)! Only massive bloodshed of non-Shiites could "revenge" Hussein's death
more than 1300 years ago!

The problem with revenge in the Muslim world is that one
never knows which event or which "affront" in the past is the
trigger for the vengeful act. Thousands of "scores" are subject to
being settled.

The violent face of Islam lies just under the surface at all times, in countless areas of the world.

Who Dies? The Young!

To a Muslim, dying and killing for the cause of Islam is not only an honor and a way of bringing "glory" to a person's family, it is a way of pleasing Allah. In fact, the *only* way Muslims can have a hope for paradise is by becoming a martyr for the cause of Islam. The quickest way to paradise is to engage in activity that is in direct opposition to infidels.

In preparing to wage war against Iraq, Khomeini called for ten thousand volunteers to fight. Thousands of young boys stepped forward to become *basiji* ("the mobilized"). A *basiji* is not only committed to the possibility of death—he is committed to *die*. The *basijis* volunteered to clear the minefields with their bodies, and they did so. Military leaders sent out as many as five thousand boys at once to run through the fields and trip the mines.

Sometimes they asked the boys to clear high voltage border fences by throwing their bodies against the fences. Thousands of young bodies were shattered and electrocuted. Many of these boys were only twelve or thirteen years old. To them, Khomeini held out the same promise that is held out to suicide terrorists throughout the Muslim world today: "paradise" (*behesht*). Each boy was given a key to hang around his neck—it was called the key that could open the gate of heaven. One young Iranian soldier, Mohsen Naeemi, who died in the war with Iraq, left behind a note that read in part:

> My wedding is at the front and my bride is martyrdom. The sermon will be uttered by the roar of guns. I shall attire myself in my blood for this ceremony. My bride, martyrdom, shall give birth to my son, freedom. I leave this son in your safekeeping. Keep him well. (Wright, *Sacred Rage*, 44–45)

Many people in the West try to separate the grim and merciless acts of Khomeini, and others who followed his blood-splattering methodology, from the tenets of Islam. A number of scholars and writers have made this same vain attempt. The label they use is generally along the lines, "an extremist version of Islam." What these idealists fail to recognize is that violence and bloodshed are not exclusive to the Shiites, and they are not exclusive to any one nation or region. Muslim violence in the Middle East and North Africa is marked by deeds almost identical to those of the Islamic revolution in Iran.

The Muslim Brotherhood in Egypt and Syria trained a number of the initial group of Arab Palestinians to fight against Israel. The motto of this group was: "The Koran is our constitution, the Prophet is our guide; Death for the glory of Allah is our greatest ambition." (Dilip Hiro, *Holy Wars: The Rise of Islamic Fundamentalism* [New York: Routledge, 1989], 63)

The former Egyptian Interior Minister, Ahmed Mortade al Maraghi, once wrote about how young militants were recruited by the Muslim Brotherhood:

> A small room lit with candle light and smoky with incense is chosen . . . Once the likely young man is selected, he is brought to this room . . . where he will find a sheikh repeating verses from the Koran . . . The Sheikh with eyes like magnets stares at the young man who is paralyzed with awe . . . They will then pray, and the sheikh will recite verses from the Koran about those fighting for the sake of Allah and are therefore promised to go to heaven. "Are you ready for martyrdom?" the young man is asked. "Yes, yes," he repeats. He is then given the oath on the Koran. These young men leave the meeting with one determination: to kill. (Wright, *Sacred Rage*, 179)

A number of terrorism-oriented groups have sprung from the Muslim Brotherhood, including Al Jihad ("The Jihad Organization") and Al Taqfir Wal Higrah ("Repentance and Migration"). Hundreds of innocent people have been targeted and killed by these groups. Hamas, Hezbollah, Amal, and the Palestinian Liberation Organization (PLO) have all taken cues from the Muslim Brotherhood.

Bernard Lewis, one of the great scholars of Islam, has written:

> "There is something in the religious culture of Islam which inspired, in even the humblest peasant or peddler,

a dignity and a courtesy toward others never exceeded and rarely equaled in other civilizations. And yet, in moments of upheaval and disruption, when the deeper passions are stirred, this dignity and courtesy toward others can give way to an explosive mixture of rage and hatred which impels even the government of an ancient and civilized country—even the spokesman of a great spiritual and ethical religion—to espouse kidnapping and assassination, and try to find, in the life of their prophet, approval and indeed precedent for such actions." (Quoted in Andrew Sullivan, "This *Is* a Religious War" *New York Times Magazine* October 10, 2001)

Rewards for the Martyrs—from a Glorious Status to 72 Virgins in Glory. Those who die for the cause of Islam are heralded as martyrs. Their photographs are often enlarged to massive poster size and hung in village squares or posted on the sides of buildings.

The photographs of suicide bombers are routinely shown to school children, beginning in kindergarten. The suicide bombers are called heroes and young boys are asked to imagine themselves attaining the glory of these heroes.

The rewards are not only in terms of reputation. There's money to be gained.

Most Westerners seem unaware that Iraqi President Saddam Hussein sends the Iraqi-funded Arab Liberation Front to the door of a Palestinian suicide bomber's home with a check for $10,000. More than three hundred of these checks have been issued and Saddam Hussein has pledged almost a billion dollars to support the Intifada, the Palestinian uprising.

Suicide bombers are told in advance of their deeds that when they die, their families will be exalted. Although the families may appear to mourn at a funeral publicly, privately they celebrate a wedding. Why? Because when the bomber arrives in Paradise, there are seventy-two virgins supposedly waiting for him, ready to fulfill his every sexual fantasy.

This appeal, of course, is a strong one for a young boy just entering puberty, just as it remains strong for those in their later teen years and early twenties—especially if they see nothing positive in their future.

We must not lose sight of the fact that the majority of the world's Muslims today are under the age of twenty-five. They are living in societies in which the leaders exert a total ideological and economic stranglehold on the people, without many possibilities for a decent education or a good job. The sale of illegal drugs and gun-running are mainstays in the economies of a number of Muslim nations. These youths are ripe for the message of the most bigoted and intolerant of the Muslims, who openly advocate violence as a means of liberation from Western values and a more prosperous, equitable life.

Chapter Six

THE GOAL OF A WORLD EMPIRE

Islamic fundamentalism and the goal of a world empire have been on the rise for the last twenty-five years.

Islamic fundamentalism, however, did not begin with Khomeini. It began in the seventh century.

Islam experienced a phenomenal expansion under the second caliph (successor), Omar (634–644). Muslim armies defeated the armies of the Sassanian (Persian) and Byzantine empires. Muslims swept through the area that is present-day Iraq and Iran to Central Asia (Bukhara and Samarkand) and the Punjab of India. They conquered all Asiatic territories of the Roman Empire except Anatolia (modern Turkey). Moving northward they occupied Syria. Damascus became the capital of the Umayyad Dynasty (661–750). They conquered Egypt and moved across North Africa and into Europe, ruling most of Spain. Charles Martel at the Battle of Tours in France stopped their move into the West in 732.

Within a hundred years after Muhammad's death (632), Islam was the empire of Allah from the Pyrenees to the Punjab, from the Sahara to Samarkand.

The empire that was established in the seventh century began to collapse in some areas by the end of the tenth century. Islam then had a resurgence of growth from the fifteenth to the eighteenth centuries. Islam rose up in the form of three new and powerful empires—the Mughal in India, the Safavieh in Iran, and the Ottoman in Anatolia (Turkey). Islam spread into many new regions in Africa, Asia, and the Middle East, and many were converted to Islam.

Of particular concern to the West was the Ottoman Empire, the most aggressive of the three Islamic movements. By the end of the sixteenth century, the Ottomans had conquered several Byzantine provinces, including Greece and Bulgaria. Constantinople, long a bulwark of Christendom, fell in 1453 and became Istanbul, capital of the Ottoman Empire.

Under Suleiman the Magnificent (1520–1566) the Ottomans gained control of all the Balkan Peninsula, except Montenegro, and a strip of the Dalmatian coast. It reached into Hungary, made the Black Sea a Turkish lake, and embraced Asia Minor, the Euphrates valley, Armenia, Georgia, Syria, Palestine, Egypt, and the north coast of Africa as far as Morocco. The advance of the Ottomans was stopped at the gates of Vienna in 1529. Many areas that had been predominantly Christian became predominantly Muslim. Christian communities survived, but systematic and compulsory conversion to Islam was common. Thousands of sons of Christian parents were torn from their homes, reared as Muslims, and enrolled in the armies. Many churches were transformed into mosques.

The trouble we have seen in recent years in the former Yugoslavia (conflicts among Serbia, Croatia, Herzegovina, and Bosnia) have their roots in this Islamic invasion during the sixteenth century.

Among many Islamic groups, the terms "West" or "Christian" are not used, but rather, the term "Crusaders" (al-Salibia). To many active Islamic groups in the Middle East, the Crusades are not over! (Jews, by the way, are generally referred to as Zionists [al-Sahyouniyya], for reasons we will explain in the next chapter.)

Christianity is seen as the foremost foe of Islam. It is what stands in the way of the advancement of Islam on virtually all geographic, historical, and ideological fronts.

Christianity—Enemy Number One

How do Islamic extremists regard Christianity?

First and foremost, Islamic extremists see Christianity as an expression of infidel values and practices.

Second, Islamic extremists see Christianity as the most potent ideology they face—far more potent than other religions, communism, or atheism. If the most potent foe can be subjugated, all other foes will become simply "a mop up action."

Third, although they regard Christianity as a potent ideology, Islamic extremists tend to regard Christian people as passive "easy" targets—especially Christians who live in the democratic West, who seem to Muslims to have a "live and let live" attitude as part of the freedom of religion they enjoy in their democracies. Islamic extremists see very few defensive measures set up against their radical tactics.

Fourth, Islamic extremists see the Christian West, and primarily the United States, as being responsible for many of the "ills" experienced in the Middle East—first and foremost, the establishment of the State of Israel; second, the establishment of military bases in Saudi Arabia and other nations, and third, the introduction into the Middle East of Western culture in all its forms that are opposed to Islam.

Christians around the world have been targets in violent actions that are ongoing. Consider these news briefs from the last few years:

- Pakistan's Christian community (about two million strong in a nation with 140 million people) was targeted in 1998 riots that followed United States military retaliation against Afghanistan for attacks on U.S. embassies. Enraged Muslims killed a pastor and fifteen parishioners of a Pakistani church in Behawalpur—the attack came shortly after American military troops entered Afghanistan (October 2001).

- Radical Muslims in Indonesia are reported to have killed about ten thousand Christians in 2000–2001. A number of Christian houses and churches were burned. In all, the lives of about fifty thousand Christians are considered to be in jeopardy in the towns and villages of Indonesia's Sulawesi Island.

- Christians in Iraq—an extremely small minority—were denied food rations after the United States began its military operation in Afghanistan in October 2001.

- Muslims have waged a twenty-year "holy war" against Christians in Sudan, resulting in more than two million deaths and thirteen million refugees. Sudanese clerics have released a "fatwa" (a religious ruling) stating, "America is the greatest enemy of Islam and it embraces blasphemy, guards the Jews and protects their terrorism." (The *Charlotte World*, October 26, 2001)

- Since September 11, 2001, persecution against religious believers has intensified in Saudi Arabia, which has been classified by the United States as one of the worst violators of religious freedom in the world. The majority of the people arrested have been Christians from Africa and Asia—even though Saudi law states that non-Muslims from other nations are free to worship in private.

- At least two hundred people died during fighting between Muslim and Christian groups in Kano, Nigeria on October 13, 2001. The deaths came in a riot that followed the staging of an anti-America protest that included Islamic religious slogans and pictures of Osama bin Laden. An eyewitness claimed Christians in Muslim-dominated areas were slaughtered outright.

Consider also the actions that have been taken in the last twenty-five years as a result of militant Islamic individuals or groups moving specifically against *The United States:*

- in 1979 a group of Muslim students seized the United States Embassy in Tehran and held fifty-two Americans hostages for 444 days.

- in 1979 the U.S. Embassy in Islamabad, Pakistan, was set on fire by a group of Muslim fundamentalists.

- in 1982, thirty-seven Americans and other Westerners were taken hostage by Hezbollah in Lebanon. Hezbollah freed the last American in 1991.

- In 1983 Hezbollah conducted three suicide bomb attacks in Beirut, killing 350 people. The American Embassy, the United States military barracks, and the French military barracks were targeted. Among the dead were 241 United States Marines.

- in 1985, Hezbollah hijacked a TWA jetliner to Beirut, killing a United States Navy diver on board.

- in 1988, an Islamic group from Libya downed a Pan Am jetliner over Scotland, killing all 259 passengers bound for the United States.

- Throughout the 1980s, nearly a hundred foreigners were kidnapped in Lebanon by Hezbollah—at least eight of these hostages were killed, including three Americans.

- in 1993, a powerful bomb rocked the World Trade Center in New York City. Six people were killed and a thousand more injured. Sheik Omar Abdel Rahman and fourteen of his followers were arrested and charged with the bombing. In the aftermath of their arrests, officials uncovered plots to blow up a federal building in Manhattan, the United Nations building, the Lincoln and Holland tunnels, and the George Washington Bridge. (George J. Church, "Laying Hands on an Unwanted Guest" [*Time,* July 12, 1993], 27)

In recent years, we have witnessed the bombing of two U.S. embassies in Africa, the bombing of the USS Cole, and ultimately, violent attacks on the World Trade Center in New York City and the Pentagon in Washington, D.C.

A Hatred for Americans on "Islamic Holy Ground"

The Islamic extremists especially decry the presence of United States personnel—military and political, and to a certain extent, civilians—on what is considered to be "holy ground." In particular,

Islamic extremists are angered at what they perceive to be the American and Jewish presence in Palestine, and the American presence in Saudi Arabia.

As far back as 1981, Iranian pilgrims bound for Mecca were deported by Saudi troops for carrying posters of the Ayatollah Khomeini and tracts calling for the overthrow of the Saudi regime. The main objection of Khomeini and his followers was that the Saudis were in too close company with the United States.

With the onset of the Gulf War in the early 1990s, the people of Iran and Iraq openly decried the presence of American troops on Islamic soil.

If the animosity is so great between Islam and Christianity, why did Saudi Arabia allow Americans to come to its desert—not only at the time of the Gulf War, but with an ongoing presence? Islamic jurisprudence allows for temporary agreement with infidels if Muslims are in a state of need. Once the need passes and Muslims become strong or are no longer in need, the treaty is no longer binding and Muslims can break it.

We should not be surprised if, down the road, the Muslims of Iraq and Saudi Arabia get cozy again. The villains then would likely be the United States and Israel.

Not at Peace With Itself

One might think that given their common Muslim ties, governments of largely Muslim populations would be at peace. Not so. In 1981, a group of Shiite Muslims from several Arab states tried unsuccessfully to overthrow Bahrain's Sunni government. This act of aggression was just one act in centuries of conflict between Sunni Muslims and Shiite Muslims. In fact, much of the instability in the governments in the Middle East grows out of long-standing disputes between Sunnis and Shiites.

Following the death of Muhammad, his trusted friend Abu Bakr was named the first caliph. He had been one of the first converts to Islam, was Muhammad's close advisor, and was his father-in-law. The choice of Abu Bakr to lead the newly founded Islamic community—the *Ummah*—disappointed Ali, who was Muhammad's cousin, son-in-law, and close friend. Ali considered himself to be Muhammad's legitimate heir and successor. Ali did not assume power, however, until after two more successors, Ummar and Othman, had died.

After Ali was named Caliph, a power struggle arose and Ali was assassinated by Muawiya, founder of the Umayyad Dynasty. The caliphate passed on to the monarchical House of Umayyad.

Meanwhile, Ali's son, Hussein, claimed that as Muhammad's grandson, the caliphate belonged to him. The struggle that followed split the Muslim world into supporters of the house of Ali (and Hussein) and supporters of the House of Umayyad.

Hussein was killed in battle with Caliph Yazid of the Umayyads and upon his death, the split was permanent. Two main groups became the *Shi-at Ali*—literally "the party of Ali," which supported the descendants of Ali as rightful rulers, and the Sunni (followers of the "Prophet's Path"), supporting first the Umayyads and later the Abbasids.

The Shiites felt a deep sense of having been wronged after they were defeated by the Sunnis. James Cook wrote:

> They became dissenters, subversives within the Arab empire, given to violence against authority. Shiite Islam was an extremely emotional sect and still is. Its adherents at times clothe themselves in black cloaks and black turbans, and once a year re-enact the passion of Husayn (Hussein), sometimes flagellating themselves as a means of atoning for Husayn's (Hussein's) martyrdom. (James Cook, "Sunis? Shiites? What's That Got to Do With Oil Prices?" [*Forbes* April 12, 1982], 99)

Shiites insist that the descendants of Ali are the *Imams*, "leaders." Imams are considered to be sinless, almost infallible leaders in all spheres of life, including politics. Shiittes believe in a continuing revelation of Allah through the Imams, and therefore, the Imams are the only ones truly capable of interpreting and reinterpreting the Koran.

The Twelver Shiite sect teaches that the infant Twelfth Imam went into hiding in the ninth century and will remain hidden until the end of time, when he will return to earth as the *Mahdi* ("Messiah") to establish a millennium of perfect equity.

Twelver Shiites believe that until the Twelfth Imam returns, every true Muslim must put himself under the authority of a holy man, an *ayatollah*. This belief has given rise to a very strong clergy and a fairly rigid religious hierarchy. Ayatollahs wield enormous power.

Early in the sixteenth century, Twelver Shiism became the official religion of Persia, now called Iran. The clergy became increasingly powerful and developed a tradition of being in opposition to the political state—they believed the state owed religious obedience to them. In 1906 the Shiite clergy in Persia led a revolution that established a constitution and caused the fall of the two-hundred-year-old Qajar dynasty. They caused the rise of the first Pahlavi Shah, Reza Shar, and the fall of the second, Muhammad Shah.

In other Middle East nations, the Sunni religious authorities were more readily absorbed into political life—they became part of the civil service in Egypt, for example.

Ayatollah Khomeini played on the Twelver Shiites' expectation of the return of the Twelfth Imam, claiming to be a linear descendant of Ali and taking for himself the title of Imam. After leading the successful ouster of the shah, he recreated Iran to conform to his ideology and he built a state in which the clergy has absolute control.

Khomeini was not content in changing Iran alone. He sought to export his concept of religious government and his first step was to call for the downfall of Saddam Hussein in Iraq. To bring things to a boiling point, Khomeini declared that Saddam Hussein was Muawiya (the original antagonist of Ali fourteen hundred years ago) coming back from the grave to kill Khomeini. The result was an eight-year border war. The Shiite majority in Iraq, however, did not seem prepared for Khomeini's style of government and did not withdraw support from Hussein, perhaps out of fear.

Both nations paid a heavy toll for the conflict—not only financially but also in lives. Iran sent every able-bodied male into battle. At the Ramadi prisoner of war camp about sixty-five miles west of Baghdad, Iraq, prisoners ranged in age from thirteen-year-old boys to white-haired old men. One of the youngest prisoners described in tears how he had been given three months of training before being sent to the front line—he and his fellow "soldiers" had been told the Iraqis were all heathens and they had a holy duty to fight them.

As a result of this war, both the Iranian and Iraqi economies fell into shambles. We should not overlook the fact that Iraq was in *need* of Kuwait's oil resources to replenish its economy, and although the invasion of Kuwait was internationally proclaimed as a move to regain a part of the region that Iraq felt was rightfully its own territory, the real motive was economic.

A second strong motive for the invasion of Kuwait was rooted in Shiite-Sunni differences. Iraq has a predominantly Shiite population, and the leadership of oil-rich Saudi Arabia is Sunni. Only Kuwait stands between Iraq and Saudi Arabia geographically. Should Kuwait ever fall to Iraq, an open Shiite versus Sunni conflict seems inevitable.

Even though Khomeini is dead, a well-organized network of Khomeini-type radicals has been established throughout the Arab world as the result of his ideas and influence. Arabic tapes espousing Khomeini's ideas were distributed in almost every capital city in the Middle East. Engineer Muhammad Abdel Salam Farag, author of *The Missing Religious Duty* and one of the five accused assassins of Anwar Sadat, was influenced greatly by Khomeini's ideas.

Where does that leave us today?

In the last fifteen years, more "moderate" Sunni governments around the Persian Gulf have received increasing opposition from their Shiite populations. In response, some of these Sunni governments have become more radical in order to appease the Shiites within their borders.

The growing trend in Muslim countries around the world has been toward Islamic fundamentalist ideology, regardless of which branch of Islam is advocated. The Shiites, however, have traditionally been the more passionate opponents of all things Western and all things Christian.

Sect within a Sect: Wahhabism

The particular brand of Islam followed by Osama bin Laden and his colleagues is Wahhabism, a very austere and conservative branch of Islam supposedly founded by Abd al-Wahhab (1703–1787). Somewhat ironically, it was this branch that was instrumental in creating the Saudi monarchy, and it now seems the branch intent on bringing that monarchy down. Wahhabism fiercely opposes anything viewed as *bidaa ("modernity")*, which is an Arabic word—usually muttered as a curse—for any modernization or change that seems to deviate from the fundamental teachings of the Koran. At various times, such things as the telephone, radio broadcasts, public education for women, and music have all been declared to be *bidaa*.

The Wahhabis also believe their faith should never give up ground in any place Islam has ever conquered. Saudi Arabia was a major financial backer of the Mojahedin fighting to expel the godless communists from Afghanistan, and at one time, bin Laden was the public's poster boy for that cause.

The creation of an Islamic state along Wahhabi lines inspired fighters in Bosnia, and also the Chechen separatists. The ferocity with which the Wahhabis fight is legendary. An Arab historian in the eighteenth century wrote about the Wahhabis: "I have seen them hurl themselves on their enemies, utterly fearless of death, not caring how many fall, advancing rank after rank with only one desire—the defeat and annihilation of the enemy. They normally give no quarter, sparing neither boys nor old men." (As quoted in Neil MacFarquhar, "Bin Laden and His Followers Adhere to an Austere, Stringent Form of Islam" in *New York Times*, October 7, 2001)

Wahhabis advocate very strict punishment for offenders of the Koran: thieves have their left hand amputated, adulterers are stoned to death, murderers and sexual deviants are beheaded. Since King Abdel Aziz ibn Saud unified Saudi Arabia in 1932, the royal dynasty has had to balance the demands of modernization and the intolerance of the Wahhabis. Abd al-Wahhab is considered to be the co-founder of Saudi Arabia—the royal clan and the religious clan have intermarried for more than two centuries.

Osama bin Laden was born and raised in Saudi Arabia in a very conservative society with strict adherence to the Koran. He has openly stated for years that he abhors the alliance of the ruling Saudi family with the West, especially the allowing of hundreds of thousands of American and other foreign troops to set foot on Saudi Arabian soil. The Saudi government, in return, has declared that overt donations to Mr. Bin Laden are illegal, but he continues to receive both popular support and donations from "underground" Saudi sources.

One of the "intellectuals" who gave rise to much of the current terrorist thought and action was Sayyid Qutb. He was not Wahhabi, but rather, an Egyptian writer and activist who was executed by Egyptian authorities in the mid-1960s for inciting resistance to the regime in power. Nevertheless, his book *Signposts on the Road*, published in 1964, has been widely circulated in the Arabic-speaking world. He states, "no one is more distant than the Americans from spirituality and piety." Qutb strongly rejected democracy and nationalism as Western ideas incompatible with Islam. He was the first Sunni Muslim to find a way around the ancient prohibition against overthrowing a Muslim ruler. Basically, he declared they were no longer Muslims but infidels who allowed Western modernization.

Qutb's writings were considered a major source of inspiration to Sheik Omar Abdel Rahman, (who was convicted of conspiring in 1995 to blow up the World Trade Center, the United Nations, and other New York City landmarks), as well as Osama bin Laden. Bin Laden has taken Qutb's approach in declaring the Saudi government to be "illegitimate" because it allows American troops to walk on Saudi soil. The two people who seem to have had the greatest direct influence on bin Laden were Abdallah Azzam, a Palestinian who was killed by a car bomb in 1989, and Saf al-Hawalli, a Saudi who has been periodically jailed by Saudi authorities. Both men were steeped in the writings of Sayyid Qutb.

There is no accurate account as to the number of Muslims in Saudi Arabia who adhere to Wahhabism—estimates range from ten percent to seventy percent. At least ten of the hijackers who carried out the September 11 attacks came from Saudi Arabia and very likely were Wahhabis.

Chapter Seven

ALL ROADS LEAD TO ISRAEL

Israel is surrounded by twenty-two nations that are predominantly Muslim: Mauritania, Morocco, Algeria, Tunisia, Libya, Egypt, Sudan, Ethiopia, Eritrea, Djibouti, and Somalia in northern Africa; and Yemen, Oman, U.A.E. (United Arab Emerits), Saudi Arabia, Qatar, Bahrain, Kuwait, Jordan, Syria, Lebanon, and Iraq in the Middle East. (Iran, Afghanistan, and Pakistan are predominantly Muslim to the east of the area technically called "The Middle East.")

One would think that such a small nation as Israel would be of little consequence to such a huge geographic block of Islam. The exact opposite is the case. Israel, to the Muslim, is the "fly" in the cauldron of soup.

Today's Islamic zealots have sworn that there can be no peace with Israel. According to them, Israel is "a constant reminder of the Westerner's humiliation" of Islam.

Osama bin Laden said in his statements aired widely on October 7 and October 9, 2001:

- "We cannot accept Palestine will become Jewish."

- "To America, I say to it and to its people this: I swear by God the Great, America will never dream nor those who live in America will never taste security and safety unless we feel security and safety in our land and in Palestine."

- "We have a fair and just case. The Islamic nation more than eighty years has been suffering. The Palestinian people have been living under the Jewish and Zionist occupation. Nobody moves to help them. Here we are. This is an Arab land. This is a land that's being desecrated."

Other Al Qaeda sources have made similar statements, including this one by Sulaiman Abu Ghaith:

America must know that the storm of airplanes will not stop, and there are thousands of young people who look forward to death like the Americans look forward to life . . . . The American interests are everywhere all over the world. Every Muslim has to play his real and true role to uphold his religion and his nation in fighting, and jihad is a duty . . . . This battle is a decisive battle between atheism and faith . . . . The Americans have opened a door that will never be closed. America must know that the battle will not leave its land until America leaves our land; until it stops supporting Israel; until it stops the blockade against Iraq.(Transcribed from a tape given to *Al-Jazeera*, the leading Arabic television network, AP report from Cairo, October 10, 2001)

Egyptian President Mubarak has contended that fifty percent—on one occasion, he said eighty percent—of the terrorist incidents in the *world* can be attributed to the Palestinian-Israeli conflict.

Shock Waves in the Muslim World

The establishment of the State of Israel in 1948 not only sent shock waves among the Arab world, but the presence of a Jewish state in the Middle East continues to stand as one of the foremost reasons that militant Muslims hate the United States.

Since the United States has supported Israel from its inception, the hatred against the United States in various Arab sectors has been growing now for more than fifty years.

Middle East Muslims regard the establishment and development of Israel as a continuation of the aggressive acts of Western imperialism against Arab and Islamic lands. From this perspective, Israel was created to serve as a bridgehead of Western influence, penetration, and domination in the Middle East. Zionism was an off-shoot of imperialism. Israel was an "instrument" of the West.

Let's take a brief look at the history of this region and the documents associated with the establishment of the Jewish State of Israel.

The Balfour Declaration in 1917. During World War I, the Balfour Declaration was the price Great Britain paid to gain worldwide Jewish backing for the war effort. At that time Great Britain urgently needed every possible source of support. Russia, facing the aftermath of its own 1917 revolution, had dropped out of the war effort. Many leaders of the new anti-war leftist Soviet government were Jewish, and those in the West feared that these Jewish "co-religionists" would support the revolution rather than the Czarist regime (which was backed by the Allies). Some British leaders were even hoping to win German-Jewish support away from the German Kaiser.

Late in 1936, the English Prime Minister David Lloyd George revealed that the Zionists (those who advocated the existence of a political State of Israel), promised to rally Jewish pro-Allied sentiment if they received a commitment to establish a Jewish national home in Palestine, the territory now roughly called Israel. George said to the House of Commons, "They were helpful." (Don Peretz, *The Middle East Today* [New York: Holt, Rinehart, and Winston, 1978], 101)

The Balfour Declaration took the form of a public letter from Lord Balfour, the British Foreign Minister, to Lord Rothschild, a prominent English leader in Jewish causes. It stated:

> His Majesty's government views with favor the establishment in Palestine of a national home for the Jewish people and would use their best endeavors to facilitate the achievement of this object. It being clearly understood that nothing shall be done which may prejudice

the civil and religious rights of existing non-Jewish communities in Palestine, or the rights and political status enjoyed by Jews in any other country. (Peretz, *The Middle East Today*)

This territory named Palestine was something of an anomaly. Both the Jewish and Arab populations were among the most politically sophisticated and culturally developed in the entire Middle East in the early 1900s. Conflict between Jewish and Arab nationalism—both groups sought a political state—had frustrated all British attempts to encourage local self-government. Arab nationalists considered Palestine part of the Arab heartland and refused to surrender any of their rights or claims. Jewish Zionists, for their part, envisioned Palestine as a Jewish national home. The duplicity and devious dealings of the British in the area did not help smooth these differences. At times, the promises of the officer at the foreign office in Cairo were diametrically opposed to those of the foreign secretary in London. When British nationalists pressured British officials, they tried to stop Zionist expansion. When the Jewish lobby in Britain counter-pressured, the British leaned on the Arabs. The result was that both Arabs and Zionists were left guessing much of the time.

Britain came to feel what it called "dual obligation." On the one hand, Britain tried to accommodate to the pressure of Zionists whose power in England showed itself mainly at the ballot box, and on the other hand, they tried to appease the Arabs, whose satisfaction the British felt obligated to ensure after receiving Arab support in World War I.

Any support of the Zionist cause, of course, was regarded with great suspicion on the part of the Arab leaders, who saw this as a definite affront not only to their political aspirations, but to their religious ideals and claims.

The Origin of Zionism. Modern Zionism calls for the return of Jewish people to the "homeland"—by which Zionists refer to the ancient land of Israel as described in the Old Testament. In many ways, Zionism was a direct product of the economic, political, and social climate of nineteenth-century Europe. When Jews left Palestine following the Roman conquest of the first century, they emigrated or were transported primarily to Europe. For the most part, they formed communities separate from the Europeans and in these Jewish communities, they practiced the laws, traditions, and customs of ancient Israel.

In most countries, the Jews remained "foreigners" for centuries, in spite of their business and political involvement in various nations. They were rather frequently expelled en masse. Nearly every major European nation—Spain, France, England, Poland, Germany, Romania—exiled its Jewish community at one time or another from 70 A.D. to 1948 A.D. The famous Jewish writer and activist, Theodore Herzl, once wrote:

> The Jews would always be persecuted no matter how useful or patriotic they were. Nowhere was their integration into national life possible; the Jewish problem, the hatred of the Jewish minority by non-Jewish majority, existed wherever there were Jews. Even immigration to hopefully safe places did not exempt Jews from eventual anti-Semitism. (Peretz, *The Middle East Today*)

When the idea of a homeland became a reality in the aftermath of the horrendous Holocaust associated with World War II, thousands of remaining Jews flocked to Israel from Europe. Other Jews from around the world did as well, driven both by the "ideal" of a Jewish state and by concerns for safety and the right of religious freedom.

In 1914, some eighty-five thousand Jews were living in Palestine, as were some six thousand Arabs—in other words, Jews outnumbered Arabs 14 to 1. This population figure is often overlooked when Westerners discuss the Jewish-Arab conflict in Israel. Far more Jews have lived in this part of the world historically, and certainly throughout the last century, than have Arabs.

While Jewish sentiment was increasingly focused on the Zionist theme during the late 1800s, Arab loyalty was not politically focused. Rather, Arabs in the area expressed loyalty to either Islam or Christianity. (About five percent of the Arabs in Palestine call themselves Christians. They are descendants of converts going all the way back to the first century.)

A distinctive Arab, or later "Palestinian" common nationalist movement did not emerge until World War I. Up until World War I, Osmanlis (the people of the Ottoman Empire, or Turkey) exercised a shadowy form of control over many parts of the region. The

Bedouin still roamed the hills and valleys and periodically raided the settled villages in the hill country on the north plains.

Shortly after the outbreak of World War I, the Ottomans clamped rigid restriction on Palestine and the surrounding area. Their treatment was harsh, but so was the treatment of nature—widespread drought and a locust plague caused famine in the region.

After the Balfour Declaration, Arabs became increasingly fearful that Palestine would become wholly Jewish. Winston Churchill's white paper of July 1922 was an attempt to clarify the British position. Churchill basically affirmed two things: one, that the Balfour Declaration did not state that "Palestine as a whole should be converted into a Jewish national home, but that such a home should be found in Palestine," and two, all citizens of the country were Palestinian, and none were entitled to any special judicial status. In speaking to Jewish concerns, Churchill affirmed that the promises of the Balfour Declaration were not to be abandoned, but that those promises did not entail an imposition of Jewish nationality on all the country's inhabitants, but rather, that Britain would continue the political and economic development of the existing Jewish community, with the help of world Jewry.

San Remo Conference and League of Nations. At the time of the San Remo Conference in 1920, the area called Palestine under British mandate is the geographic area we know today as Israel and Jordan. From 1921 to 1923, Britain divided this mandated area for purposes of its own supervisory governance. Essentially, a line was drawn from the Dead Sea south to Elat (on the upper tip of the Red Sea). The Jordan River formed the boundary between the Sea of Galilee and the Dead Sea, and the Golan Heights were part of the northern area of Palestine, bordering with Syria, which was under the French Mandate. The area east of this line was called "Transjordan" and was closed to all Jewish settlement. The area to the west was designated for the Jewish national homeland.

In essence, the Arabs were given all the land east of the Jordan River, the Jews were given the land west of it.

In 1922, the League of Nations assigned the "Palestinian Mandate" to Great Britain. This mandate differed from other Middle East mandates that called for progressive development of independent states. In Palestine, the British were vested with "full powers of legislation and of administration save as they may be limited by the terms of this mandate." (P.M. Holt, *Egypt and The Fertile Crescent 1516–1922* [Ithaca and London: Cornell University Press, 1966], 292). The Lausanne Peace Treaty with Turkey in 1923 affirmed this position taken by the League of Nations. What this mandate meant was that Great Britain maintained great power over the region called Palestine.

Great Britain also was given control of Iraq, Egypt and modern Jordan. France claimed Lebanon, Syria, Algiers, Morocco, and Tunisia as part of its "mandate" from the League of Nations.

Specifically, the British mandate for Palestine authorized Jewish immigration and "closed settlement" on the land, which meant that Jews who decided to establish permanent residence could be assisted in obtaining Palestinian citizenship. Jewish leaders were authorized to construct and operate public works, services, and utilities not directly undertaken by the British "mandatory administration."

In 1923, Britain ceded the Golan Heights to the French because Britain did not want to allocate governing resources to that area and the French were already in the region. Both Jews and Syrians lived on the Golan.

Both Jewish and Arab communities complained that the British mandatory authorities discriminated against them. Both protested any measure intended to lead toward self-government of the other— the Arabs did not believe the measures were strong enough on their behalf, the Jews believed the measures appeared to favor the Arabs.

For its part, Great Britain also felt itself in danger of jeopardizing its friendship with other Muslim nations if it antagonized the Palestinian Arabs, and felt it might keep the entire region from becoming modernized and democratic if it alienated the Jewish community. Policy fluctuated on all levels and in various directions depending to a great extent on the whims and prejudices of local officials.

Bitterness grew and gaps eventually became unbridgeable. Each community pretty much went its own way, developing separate institutions that were often in violent conflict with each other.

Even though Palestinian "citizenship," a Palestinian "government," and Palestinian "officials" all existed in a formal sense, no

Palestinian "community" formed. British official life operated as it had for decades, especially in military and administrative circles. The Arab community fused Muslim and various Christian communities together under the control of leading Muslim families. Arab self-governing institutions often supplemented the functions of British mandatory government. Jewish settlement in the area continued and various communities were established, many operating under a communal "kibbutz" system.

The United Nations "Partition Plan." In 1947, the United Nations General Assembly Resolution 1981 adopted a "Partition Plan" that set aside a segment of the Galilee region, the area that has come to be called "the west bank" area, and the Gaza strip for an "Arab State," with the remaining area designated for the "Jewish State." The plan provided that Jerusalem be kept as an international zone.

Acting on this United Nations resolution, Israel declared its independence as a nation on May 1, 1948. The declaration is only one page in length. Since many have never seen this document, the Declaration is reprinted below in its entirety:

We, the members of the National Council, representing the Jewish people in Palestine and the Zionist movement of the world, met together in solemn assembly by virtue of the natural and historic right of the Jewish people and the Resolution of the General Assembly of the United Nations:

Hereby proclaim the establishment of the Jewish State in Palestine, to be called Israel.

We hereby declare that as from the termination of the Mandate at midnight, this night of the 14th to 15th of May 1948, and until the setting up of the July elected bodies of the State in accordance with a Constitution, to be drawn up by a constituent Assembly not later than the first day of October 1948, the present National Council shall act as the Provisional State Council and its executive organ, the National Administration, shall constitute the Provisional Government of the State of Israel.

The State of Israel will be open to the immigration of Jews from all countries of their dispersion; will promote the development of the country for the benefit of all its inhabitants; will be based on the precepts of liberty, justice and peace taught by the Hebrew Prophets; will uphold the full social and political equality of all its citizens, without distinction of race, creed or sex; will guarantee full freedom of conscience, worship, education and culture; will safeguard the sanctity and inviolability of the shrines and Holy Places of all religions; and will dedicate itself to the principles of the Charter of the United Nations.

The State of Israel will be ready to cooperate with the organs and representatives of the United States in the implementation of the Resolution of the Assembly of November 29, 1947 and will take steps to bring about the Economic Union over the whole of Palestine.

We appeal to the United Nations to assist the Jewish people in the building of its State and to admit Israel into the family of nations.

In the midst of wanton aggression, we yet call upon the Arab inhabitants of the State of Israel to return to the ways of peace and play their part in the development of the State, with full and equal citizenship and due representation in all its bodies and institutions, provisional or permanent.

We offer peace and amity to all the neighboring states and their peoples, and invite them to cooperate with the independent Jewish nation for the common good of all. Our call goes out to the Jewish people all over the world to rally to our side in the task of immigration and development and to stand by us in the great struggle for the fulfillment of the dream of generations — the redemption of Israel.

With trust in Almighty God, we set our hand to this Declaration, at this Session of the Provisional State Council, in the city of Tel-Aviv, on the Sabbath eve, the fifth of Iyar, 5708, the fourteenth day of May, 1948.

(Signatures followed)

The War of Independence. Within hours after the above Declaration was made public, five nations declared war on the new State of Israel and a year-long "War of Independence" began. In 1949, armistice lines were drawn that gave Egypt control of the Gaza area. The "west bank" area of Samaria and Judea was under Jordanian supervision, and the remainder of the area was declared to be Israel. Jerusalem became a divided city—east Jerusalem to the Arabs and west Jerusalem to the Jews. Jordanian control over Jerusalem included control over the entire Old City of Jerusalem, including the Temple Mount and many of the most revered Christian sites.

The Six Day War. In May 1967 Egypt moved into the Sinai militarily and ordered United Nations troops out of that area, imposed a blockade of the Straits of Tiran, and entered into alliance with Jordan. In June, military forces from Syria, Jordan, and Egypt moved simultaneously against Israel. The conflict became known as the "Six Day War." After Israel had successfully repulsed this attack, the cease-fire lines this time gave Israel control of the Golan Heights, the west bank, Gaza, and the Sinai. The Straits of Tiran were opened and Jerusalem was united under Israeli control.

The government of Israel subsequently annexed the Golan Heights (which had only been under Syrian control for nineteen years, during which time more than four hundred attacks had been launched against the Galilee region). Israel also annexed east Jerusalem. The remaining areas were not annexed, but were patrolled and controlled by an "occupation force" to ensure that no further assaults were launched against Jews in the region.

The Yom Kippur War. In 1973, while the vast majority of Jewish citizens, including soldiers, were at Yom Kippur services, Egypt and Syria launched simultaneous attacks against Israel. Egyptian tanks crossed the Suez and Syrian tanks moved into the Golan. The Israel Defense Force (IDF) not only turned the tide of the attack, but crossed the Suez Canal into Egypt, and IDF forces advanced to within twenty miles of Damascus. Brezchnev, leader of the Soviet Union at the time, threatened to enter the war with Soviet military forces at that point and a cease-fire was reached within three weeks after the initial attack. Israel withdrew to its 1967 borders, not making any claim to the areas it had "taken" in Egypt and Syria. Both Jewish and Arab forces suffered a heavy loss of life.

The Arab Perspective: "A Mistreated People"

The British role in creating the State of Israel and later, America's recognition of Israel, left a deep scar in the Arab Muslim world. Arabs, and in particular Muslim activists, felt certain that the Christian West had implanted Israel in their midst to exert control over the Middle East. They had recurring fears that yet another Crusade had been launched against Islam.

Muslims, unlike Westerners, cannot forget the past easily. To them, the Crusades of the Middle Ages happened yesterday. To them, colonialism still exists—and particularly, with the establishment of Israel. Most Muslim activists deeply resent the British and the French for "dividing" the Arab nations between them like a loaf of bread after World War I. The end result is that Muslims regard Israel as a direct affront to their claim to the area and an act of disrespect for the dignity of the Arab people. These are not just wild accusations. They are deeply held convictions.

The thought that "the House of War"—the Muslim identity for non-Muslims—should occupy a land that once belonged in their minds to the House of Islam, is no small matter to Muslims in general. It strikes at the very heart of Islamic ideology.

In short, the Muslims will not rest until the Jews either leave "Palestine" or accept rulership by a Muslim government.

Establishment of the PLO. The Palestine Liberation Organization (PLO) was formed specifically to "liberate all of Palestine" and place it under Arab rule. PLO headquarters initially were in Jordan, but Jordan expelled the PLO in 1970 and the PLO moved to Lebanon. Yasir Arafat rose to prominence during that transition time.

The Oslo Accord. The Oslo Accord—the agreement struck between Israel's prime minister Yitzak Rabin (with great input from Shimon Peres) and Yasir Arafat—created the Independent Palestinian Authority (IPA). The IPA was given jurisdiction over Gaza and Jericho, and in subsequent years, has been given governmental authority over Ramallah, Bethlehem, and several other cities and areas. Arafat has demanded, and continues to demand, the whole of the west bank—including those areas settled by Jews and "cultivated" as farms by Jews (farms that provide food for both Arabs and Jews). He also demands the whole of the "old city" of Jerusalem.

The Heart of the Region: Jerusalem

Within the context of the greater history of Israel, it is worth noting the specific history of Jerusalem.

Jerusalem has been considered the international capital city of the Jewish people since King David gained control of the city in 1996 B.C.—more than four thousand years ago. Jewish people have lived in the city continually since even before that final conquest by King David.

Jerusalem in Muslim History. Jerusalem is not mentioned in the Koran, and the name "Jerusalem" does not figure in early Muslim writings. When the city is mentioned at all, it is called Aelia, the name imposed by the Romans to obliterate its Jewish and Christian associations.

While the *city* is not mentioned, the al-Aqsa mosque on the Temple Mount is mentioned several times in the "sayings" of Muhammad. Muhammad supposedly declared:

- the reward or blessing for a Muslim who prayed in the al-Aqsa mosue was multiplied five hundred times
- the al-Aqsa mosque was the second mosque established on earth
- Muslims should not undertake difficult journeys except to reach three destinations, the al-Haram mosque in Mecca, the prophet's mosque in Medina, and al-Aqsa mosque in Jerusalem.

The Koran refers to God taking Muhammad on a journey by night from the mosque in Mecca to the al-Aqsa mosque. The journey ended with Muhammad ascending directly into heaven from the rock now located in the Dome of the Rock shrine.

The Dome of the Rock. The Dome of the Rock was built by Abd al-Malik on the Temple Mount in Jerusalem in 692 A.D. It was the first great religious building complex in the history of Islam and marked the beginning of a new era. It was a declaration to the world that Islam was to be the supreme religion of the world. This verse of the Koran figured prominently in the design of the building: "There is no God but God alone, he has no companion. Muhammad is the Prophet of God, who sent him with guidance the religion of truth to make it prevail over all religion." (9:33)

The Crusades and Following—Various Groups in Control. Following the Crusader entry into Jerusalem in 1099, all Jews in the City were either murdered, sold into slavery in Europe, or ransomed to the Jewish community of Egypt. The Crusaders then brought in Christian Arab tribes from east of the Jordan River and settled them in the Old City. The Templum Domini was erected over the sacred stone on the Temple Mount.

Praying for the Peace of Jerusalem

What should be our response as Christians?

First, we must voice our concern that Christian sites in Israel be protected, and that the rights of Christians, in both Israel and in the areas controlled by the IPA, be honored.

Second, we must continue to support Gospel missions to both Jews and Muslims—for both desperately need to hear that He is the only hope for peace.

Third, we need to become informed about the historical and modern-day events in Israel and Jerusalem. We need to speak the truth any time we hear lies.

And fourth, more than ever, we need to heed the admonition of the psalmist and pray for the peace of Jerusalem:

> May those who love you be secure.
>> May there be peace within your walls
>> and security within your citadels.
> For the sake of my brothers and friends,
>> I will say, "Peace be within you."
>> For the sake of the house of the LORD our God,
>> I will seek your prosperity. (Ps. 120:6–9]

Chapter Eight

OIL—THE FUEL THAT FUNDS

The world economy continues to be driven by oil. The West is dependent upon oil for its manufacturing (heavy crude) and for its transportation (lighter crude oil and refined oils, including gasoline).

The United States is the world's largest importer of foreign oil. As much as some American economists might like to deny it, America has become dependent on a system that, to a great degree, can bring the world's strongest economy to its knees. As long ago as the mid-seventies, the United States was importing f its oil needs. Just a decade before, America welve percent of its daily requirements.

today imports 53 percent of its oil, most of ers. The Persian Gulf states are predicted to he world's oil by 2010, raking in more than the process.

billion barrels of oil and 10 trillion cubic ce 1998, the United States has increased ne hundred percent.

e to 259 billion barrels of oil and 204 tril-al gas.

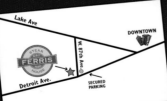

All told, some 696 billion barrels of oil could potentially be at stake if the strikes against militant Islam in Afghanistan break out into neighboring nations.

The world's oil dependency has resulted in fantastic wealth flowing into Muslim nations, virtually overnight. That certainly is the case in the Arab oil-producing nations. Those nations belonging to the Organization of Petroleum Exporting Countries (OPEC) saw their profits skyrocket from $50 billion in 1974 to $200 billion in 1980, and in just one decade, to more than $1 trillion. In 1981, Saudi Arabia earned $110 billion from the sale of oil. In 1990, with the price of a barrel reaching nearly $40, the profits staggered the imagination of both those who were paying for the oil and those who were receiving the payment.

What an interesting dynamic we have created for ourselves in the West! We show no signs of lessening our dependence on foreign oil. We seem willing to pay more and more for it. And yet, an oil shortage or oil "crisis" can trigger major upheaval in our economy.

Muslim Beliefs Related to Oil

The West may flood OPEC nations with geologists, petroleum engineers, economists, and diplomats, but until these "experts" come to grips with Islamic ideology, their understanding of the Middle East oil picture will only be partial.

Two basic Islamic beliefs are closely related to the issues associated with money and oil.

A Sign of God's Pleasure. Economic success is regarded by Muslims as a sign of God's pleasure. Prior to the rise in oil consumption, and increased drilling in Muslim nations, the Muslims tended to measure Allah's blessing by whether a war was won or lost. Muslims from the very beginning have held to a belief that Allah "reveals" the weaknesses of other faiths—therefore, a victory in war was regarded as a revelation of weakness on the part of the nation or people defeated. And since most of these nations held to a belief system other than Islam, military victories were seen as a victory authorized by Allah for the advancement of Islam.

Beginning with the Battle of Badr in 624 A.D., victories of war were regarded as "proof" of divine support. This conviction deepened during Islam's first millennium (600 A.D. to 1600 A.D.) as Islam spread over the Middle East, North Africa, and as far west as Spain.

In the last several decades, Islam has interpreted financial success as evidence of Allah's blessings on Islamic advances. This belief is one of the reasons that even so-called moderate Muslims, as embarrassed as they were by Khomeini's excesses during the Iranian revolution, would not totally disown him. The economic success of Iran under his leadership was "proof" to most in the Islamic world that Khomeini enjoyed the "pleasure" of Allah.

A Means of Gaining World Superiority. Oil is also regarded by many in the Islamic world as a material gift from Allah so Muslims (and Islam as a religion) might achieve world superiority. J.B. Kelly, the author of *Arabia, the Gulf and the West*, has written:

> The Arabs see the oil weapon as a gift sent by God to redress the balance between Christendom and Islam . . . and to fulfill the destiny which God in His infinite wisdom has ordained for those to whom He has chosen to reveal the one true faith. Extravagant though these fancies may appear to Western eyes, they are very real to those who entertain them, and infinitely more appealing than the calmer dictates of reason. (J.B. Kelly, "Islam Through the Looking Glass," *The Heritage Lectures* [Washington: The Heritage Foundation, 1980], 8)

Oil in the twenty-first century is tantamount to the sword of the seventh century. It is a means of exerting the greatest possible force on non-Muslim adversaries. The line of thinking is basically this:

> Economic success is proof of God's favor . . .
> Success results in Islamic superiority . . .
> Other religions and cultures must be subjugated . . .
> Oil has been given by Allah as a means of controlling the Christian West by humiliating it.

Oil as a Weapon

OPEC began using the oil weapon in 1973 as a punitive measure against those nations which supported Israel in the Yom Kippur War. The oil embargo of OPEC resulted in a 366 percent increase in oil prices. Basically, oil jumped from $3 a barrel to $12 a barrel, with the total world energy bill rising to $20 billion in

1973 and $100 billion by 1976. The exorbitant cost of oil dealt a harsh blow to the world's major economies, including loss of a half million jobs and a worldwide decrease of GNP that amounted to nearly $20 billion.

After the Iranian Revolution in 1979, the price went from $12 to $24 a barrel. After the Iraqi invasion of Kuwait in 1990, the price climbed to more than $35 a barrel.

One can only guess what might happen in today's economy.

Some analysts have predicted that if OPEC cuts oil shipments to the United States, oil could go as high as $100 a barrel. The truth is, American citizens are already paying that price in the form of federal taxes. The United States spends $50 to $60 billion a year in foreign aid and military operations aimed at keeping peace in the Middle East—all so oil can move smoothly through the Persian Gulf. The United States spent $61 billion on the Gulf War. Congress has authorized $30 billion to fight terrorism and $70 billion to stimulate the economy after September 11. Our dependency on oil is expensive!

Where Does the Oil Money End Up?

What have the Arabs done with the money earned from their oil fields? If you only read the sensational press, you would think the *nouveau riche* oil barons have done little but indulge their whims. Many of the tales have been outrageous and amusing— from the Saudi Arabian princes who casually gamble away millions in a single evening in European casinos, to the sheik who tried to buy the Alamo as a birthday present for his son.

For the most part, the sparsely populated Arab member states in OPEC invested enormous amounts of their oil money in domestic development programs—from schools to housing to road systems. They soon ran out of such uses, however, for their vast treasuries. In the end, much of the money has been and continues to be channeled into foreign investment. These investments are primarily in oil-consuming nations. At latest count, Saudi Arabia was estimated to have more than a trillion dollars invested in other countries—accurate figures, however, are hard to come by since the Saudis keep much of their information extremely private.

The largest portion of surplus oil money has been invested in the United States, usually behind two or three layers of companies and negotiators to conceal the source of the money. And since the United States government does not know how much Arab money is involved in its economy, it has no means for adequately identifying or controlling those investments.

The general Arab rule is to keep financial holdings just below the level at which disclosure to the United States Securities and Exchange Commission is required. That's what the Kuwaitis did, for a number of years. Few Americans know that at one time, Kuwaitis had nearly five percent ownership in some of America's top firms. (See "Arab Banks Grow," *Business Week*, October 6, 1980, 70–84.)

It is somewhat ironic in light of what is currently happening in Washington, D.C., to recall that from 1975 to 2000, U.S. political administrations have been nervous enough about Arab investments to refuse publication or incisive analyses of Arab holdings in the United States. The White House often claimed that disclosure would scare off other Arab investors. In truth, what might have happened would have been that American investors would have been scared all the way to their toes!

Why the great secrecy?

First, the wealthy nations, such as Saudi Arabia and Kuwait, recoil at the idea that the more radical nations might know their business. The more radical nations, of course, tend to also be the poorer nations.

Second, Arab investors simply do not want the West to panic over the apparent invasion of Muslim economic influence into the Western marketplace.

This Arabic economic offensive is even more alarming in my opinion than any "oil crisis" that may have occurred or that may lie ahead. The rise in Arab investments is a far more hidden and controlling danger.

Muslim Money in Many Sectors of American Business and Government. In the past, Arab oil money has been loaned in amounts of billions of dollars to such U.S. corporations as American Telephone and Telegraph (AT&T), International Business Machines (IBM), Dow Chemical, and Kimberly-Clark. ("Arab Banks Grow," *Business Week*, October 6, 1980, 71)

Arab oil money has been invested in American real estate, apartments, hotels, shopping centers, tourist resorts, land, banks, and various financial institutions.

Arab oil money has been offered in the form of loans to major U.S. firms, including Lockheed (the aerospace giant).

Much of OPEC investment in America is in the United States government itself. A significant amount of OPEC investment has been in United States Treasury securities.

It is little wonder that former political officials—including those involved in the State Department and Defense Department—have become consultants to OPEC nations after they left political service. There are big dollars to be earned for helping OPEC investors find suitable places to put their wealth.

It should also be no surprise that those who pay are those who have the potential for altering policy on critical issues. The old adage, "follow the money" is true. We know in hindsight that when the Saudis felt Iraq could function as a buffer against the radical Iranian revolutionaries, they used their influence to push the United States to support Iraq in the Iran-Iraq war. When the tides changed and the Saudis felt Iraq was a threat to them—Kuwait being all that was standing in the path of the Iraqis' push to the south—the Saudis were quick to support American efforts against their former ally and Arab brother, Iraq.

(A little publicized fact of interest is that the main source of funding for the Taliban in Afghanistan was the Saudi Arabian *government*, not so much as an economic or political move, but as an appeasement to more radical voices in Saudi Arabia.)

At what point could Arab governments make threats of financial and oil disruption that, if carried out, would severely damage the economies of the United States and other Western nations? What pressure might be brought to bear on companies doing business with, or largely owned by, Arab governments? What might the result be if Arab money was suddenly withdrawn from American financial institutions and corporations? Those are questions worthy of serious consideration.

The Dangerous Concept of *Ummah*

Ummah is the Islamic concept of the "community of believers." In many ways, ummah is the philosophy that keeps OPEC nations united when it comes to the pricing of oil and to investment decisions.

For decades, Muslim leaders have flirted with the idea of having a "common market" built on the ummah philosophy.

Whereas Europe's common market exists for trade, however, a common market in the Arab world is likely to be one used as a religious and political tool. The first person to openly espouse this idea was Gamal Abdel Nasser of Egypt.

For the most part, *ummah* has functioned as a way for oil-rich nations to preserve their wealth. Radical Muslims would like to see a common market exist so that all the wealth of the Arab world was shared with more equity. The rich Muslims, however, want a common market only if it helps ensure the protection of their personal fortunes.

A common market requires more than OPEC. It requires a centralized banking system.

What is the danger in this? It lies in the politicizing of the banking system—or in other words, the close ties between the banks and the Arab governments. Many U.S. corporations are partially owned by Arab investors. In some cases, these investors are actually "investment banks," such as the Kuwait Investment Office or the Saudi Arabian Monetary Agency. The result is that other *nations* are actually part owners of American companies. Should these nations form an alliance, the result would be that a *block of nations* would likely assume part ownership of leading American firms.

The political ramifications are enormous—at what point does the Arab world as a whole begin to dictate American economic policy, influence economic trends, and stall American production that it views as "polluting" to Islam?

A European banker once observed, "It took the Arabs ten years to learn how to wield their oil power, but it isn't going to take that long to wield their money power." (J.B. Kelly, "Islam Through the Looking Glass," *The Heritage Lectures* [Washington: The Heritage Foundation, 1980], 8). He was right. The Arabs caught on very quickly.

Not Answerable to Non-Muslims. A related concept deeply rooted in Islamic thought is this: No Muslim should be answerable to a non-Muslim.

What happens, then, in a company where the controlling interest suddenly falls into Muslim hands? And isn't that the intent of Muslim investment—to gain control so that no Muslim is answerable to a non-Muslim?

What happens if top management is replaced with Muslim personnel who are accountable only to one another in the corporation?

It is not inconceivable to envision the day when a company might require its personnel to convert to Islam to win a Middle Eastern contract.

The West makes a keen separation between business and religion. Those in the OPEC nations do not.

We must remember always that one of the ways of subjugating a non-Muslim is to humiliate him. Certainly one form of humiliation is to instigate practices that result in inflation and large budget deficits, which in turn inconvenience and oppress Western nations and force acknowledgement that the nations are dependent upon foreign oil.

We also must remain clear on a second point: The Islamic vision for a holy war will not be deterred by external circumstances, such as the price of oil. Certainly the price of oil can help Islamic leaders to accomplish their mission, but a temporary gain or loss of income will not slow the majority in the Islamic world from carrying out their mission to chip away at Christianity and the influence of the United States around the world. Even if we become totally independent from foreign oil, the threat of radical Islam will continue.

Chapter Nine

THE SPREAD OF ISLAMIC WILDFIRE

Khomeini declared six months after he had taken over power of Iran:

> The governments of the world should know that Islam cannot be defeated. Islam will be victorious in all the countries of the world, and Islam and the teachings of the Koran will prevail all over the world. (Robin Wright, *Sacred Rage: The Wrath of Militant Islam*).

Khomeini was only voicing what has been voiced for centuries, and what continues to be voiced by radical Muslims today.

We must never be so naïve as to assume that the Muslim zone of influence is limited to the Middle East. It is a worldwide influence. Muslims are the predominant power in Indonesia, the world's fourth largest nation (population), and they are an increasing force in the Philippines. Both are economic powerhouses in Southeast Asia. Both have adherents who see clearly the "big picture" of world domination, beginning with domination of the Orient.

Growing and Building at a Rapid Pace

Muslims are on track in making Islam the world's largest religion. Muslims are currently winning fifty million people annually to their faith. (Herbert Buchsbaum, "Islam in America" *Scholastic Update* [October 22, 1993], 15)

Muslims are building mosques at an unprecedented rate in world history.

Muslim extremists are also on the rise, not decline, in most Arab nations, regardless of the supposed "crackdown" on terrorist organizations in recent months.

Let me give you the example of England.

England went from having *one* mosque in 1945 to having more than *one thousand* by 1989. Great Britain presently has more Muslims than Baptists and Methodists combined.

In the 1980s, Mirza Khizar Bakht, the secretary-general of the First Interest-Free Finance Consortium—Great Britain's Islamic bank—voiced a dream of establishing a Muslim shopping center in central London's Regent Street or in Knightsbridge. The aim of the center was to "unite the whole Muslim world in London."

If you have been to London recently, you can see that his dream has largely become a reality. Arab money and Arab influence is in full display on the streets of London. The Islamic Council of Europe, which is based in London, spends large sums on propaganda among Muslims and Christians, and has built mosques in each major European city. The Central Mosque in London has a minaret that competes with the city's cathedrals on the city's skyline. The mosque was built at an estimated cost of millions of dollars and seats 2,800 people. It is only one of hundreds of mosques that have been constructed in England, largely in the last thirty years.

While London is a major base of operations for the expansion of Islam in Europe, the greatest numbers of European Muslims live on the Continent. France has the leading Muslim population—well over three million. Muslims are the nation's second-largest religious group in France (Roman Catholic is the largest)—there are more Muslims than members of all Protestant denominations combined.

West Germany follows with more than two million. Spain has a growing number of Muslims, as does Italy. In Rome, a new mosque was constructed at an estimated cost of $20 million.

According to an ABC News report, more than five thousand mosques were built in the southern republics of the former Soviet Union within two years after the Soviet Union collapsed.

In Kenya, Muslims are currently building mosques so that one mosque can be found in every ten square kilometers, whether there are any Muslims living in that area or not.

Expansion in the United States

Islam has expanded with great fervor in the United States in the last century—the Muslim population has grown exponentially since 1960. In the decade of the '70s alone, Islam grew by 400 percent in the United States. Today, the number of Muslims in America is estimated at more than four million—some estimate the number as high as six million since the number continues to increase rapidly.

The three main reasons for this rapid growth are:

1. Increased Immigration. Since the ratification of the 1965 Immigration Act by President Lyndon Johnson, waves of Muslim immigrants have flocked to the United States. Several hundred thousand Afghan refugees who had fought Communists fled persecution and war and came to America. More than two million Iranians, the majority of them highly educated and financially well off, fled Iran. Lebanese and people from the former Yugoslavia, made their way to America to escape civil wars in their homelands. The majority of these people sought political freedom; the majority of them were also Muslims.

2. Large Families. Muslim families have high birth rates, especially the Muslims of the Middle East. Muslim parents generally are very diligent in passing on the teachings of Islam to their children.

3. Growing Popularity of Islam Among Blacks. A significant number of African Americans have converted to Islam since the 1960s. Many were blacks who rejected the values and ideals they considered outgrowths of a hypocritical white Christian society. Repeatedly the claims have been made, "Christianity is a racist religion; Islam is a religion of peace." Nothing could be more contrary to historical fact, but this has become the predominant *thought* in the minds of many black Muslims in America. You only need to listen to Louis Farrakhan for a few minutes to verify this thinking!

Overall, some sixty to ninety percent of all *converts* to Islam in the United States are African American. Sadly, eighty percent of these converts were raised in the church. In 1994, an article published in *Christianity Today* predicted, "If the conversion rate continues unchanged, Islam could become the dominant religion in Black urban areas by the year 2020." (Andres Tapia, "Churches Wary of Inner-city Islamic Inroads," *Christianity Today* [January 10, 1994], 36)

One sociologist has noted that in the 1960s when Eastern religions first became popular in the United States, the rich turned to Zen Buddhism and the poor turned to Islam. Basically the rich were seeking enlightenment, knowing that riches brought no spiritual satisfaction. The poor were attracted to power, believing that power could bring all forms of satisfaction.

The Black Muslim movement in America started during the days of segregation—the movement took strength, in part, because Blacks saw the Islamic movement as standing against oppression and as a means of restoring dignity to Black people. Not only was the Nation of Islam started during this period, but also the Five Percenters, Ansaar Allah, Islamic Party of North America, Dar ul-Islam, Islamic Brotherhood, and the Hanafi Movement.

Most Black Muslims did not turn to Islam because they were attracted to its laws or history. Rather, they were attracted to Islam because they felt powerless and Islam is a religion that advocates power and association with a "brotherhood" of power.

In the current decade, the popularity of Islam is growing dramatically in our nation's prisons, and again, Blacks are the ones who seem especially drawn to the religion. The prison population seems ideally "ripe" for the promise of power and prestige held out by Islam.

The Black Muslims in the United States have only marginally integrated with the wider community of Orthodox Islam. The American movement has taken the title of "World Community of Islam in the West." Historically, Orthodox Islam did not recognize Black Muslim Americans because of their belief in black supremacy and "other heresies." Recently, however, that has all changed.

Who Is Targeted for Conversion?

American converts to Islam seem to fall largely within the twenty- to thirty-something age group. Since the late sixties, several important Islamic organizations have been established to strengthen and support American Muslims, and to propagate their message and the practice of their faith, especially among youth and college-age students. The Council of Imams trains local mosque prayer leaders, and the Association of Muslim Students has at least two hundred active chapters on college campuses in the United States. Similar organizations can be found in England, Australia, Canada, and other Western nations.

The priorities of these organizations have been clearly stated:

- disseminate Islam through publications geared to both Muslims and non-Muslims
- establish Islamic institutions, including places of worship, community service centers, and educational facilities
- assist Muslims in practical aspects of religious observance (the five pillars of Islam)
- propagate and facilitate Islam's faith-sharing effort among non-Muslims
- encourage the "unity of Muslim conscience" through a heightened sense of belonging and Muslim identity

Vast sums of money have been made available to Islamic Americans to pursue these goals.

These organizations are far from passive. They are highly aggressive in the building of facilities and the publishing of newspapers that espouse Islamic teachings.

Which is of greater danger—the economic push for greater investment and control of American companies, or the ideological push for greater control of American minds and hearts? I contend that the latter is far more dangerous. One of the main dangers is that Islam ultimately does *not* allow for the very force that is allowing its forward surge in the United States: freedom of religion.

In the End—NO Freedom of Religion

We in America are so accustomed to religious freedom that we assume that all faiths acknowledge the viability and worthiness of other religions. That simply is not the case. Islam does *not* allow differences of belief.

Arab Islamic nations consider Christian missionary activity to be a crime and those involved in it are punished as criminals.

Numerous Muslims who converted to Christianity in North Africa and in the Middle East are languishing in prisons even as I write. Their crime? Not converting to Christianity—but rather, forsaking Islam. Forsaking what Muslims consider the only true religion is an offense punishable not only by imprisonment, but sometimes by death. There simply is no tolerance in Islam, although many so-called "moderate" Muslims might say so in order to mask the ultimate intent of the organizations in which they are involved.

We in the West need to recognize clearly that when a nation becomes "Islamic" by law—declaring itself to be an Islamic State—the native people of that land who are of any religion other than Islam suddenly become second-class citizens.

Not only do non-Muslims suffer, but also three other situations tend to arise, and to arise rather quickly:

1. A Purging of Personal Freedom. Once Muslims gain political control of an area, they move quickly to eliminate personal freedoms—especially the freedom of speech and association—as well as all external signs of non-Muslim culture.

Reports from Afghanistan have documented that within a matter of months after the Taliban secured power in Afghanistan, music and videos all but disappeared from the marketplace, schooling for women was abolished, traditional dress codes were required, including full covering for women in public, beards and head covering for men; and media reports were limited to government sanctioned news stories.

As recently as January 2002, a Muslim Brotherhood leader, Essam el-Erian, said this about the move toward more zealous Islam in Egypt: "We're still a long way off from achieving our aim of an Islamic state, but we have succeeded to a large extent in changing the fabric of society toward religious piety except for a minority that's still hung up on Western values." (Associated Press, Hamza Hendawi, "Muslim Group Gurgles under Egyptians—Brotherhood Vying Against Mubarak for Egypt's Heart" January 6, 2001).

Let me remind you of the situation in Saudi Arabia.

Few Americans seem to be aware that the nearly 400,000 American soldiers of Operation Desert Shield were told very plainly that if they wanted to celebrate religious holidays, they were to do so in remote areas where the local citizens could not observe them. Chaplains, both Christian and Jewish, were told not to wear any religious symbols in public (including head covering for Jews and crosses for Christians). There are no Christian churches or synagogues, of course, in the whole nation of Saudi Arabia. In fact, the Saudi government refuses to permit a *single room in a single building* to be used by Christians for Christian worship within Saudi Arabia.

Saudi Arabia is considered to be the "holy land" of Islam— the land of "pure Islam." Any icon of another religion is considered an abomination. The practice of an infidel is considered to be an offense to Muslims.

What an irony! American soldiers were in Saudi Arabia to help defend this nation and its enormous wealth, yet Islamic intolerance to Christians and Jews is as severe as in the days of Muhammad 1400 years ago.

Let me also remind you of the reign of terror against Christians by Idi Amin, former ruler of Uganda. Amin slaughtered an estimated 300,000 Christians before he was overthrown—once out of power, he slipped out of Uganda and ran to the protective arms of his Muslim brothers in Libya and Saudi Arabia. There, Amin was applauded by many in the Islamic world for precisely what he had done, since his massacre of Christians was seen as a forward move for Islam in Uganda.

2. An End to Innovation. Islamic rule in most of the world has resulted in a halt to technology and modernization in general.

Apart from the oil-producing nations, the nations in which Islam dominates are not wealthy nations. Wealth in the modern world has been strongly linked to modernization, and Islam as a whole stands against innovation, creativity, and modernization. There is a saying attributed to Muhammad, although it is not in the Koran: "The worst things are those that are novelties. Every novelty is an innovation, every innovation is an error, and every error leads to Hellfire." Sunni Islam defines observance of tradition as good, departure from tradition as bad.

Enough innovation has trickled into the Islamic world to show poor Muslims that they do *not* have the conveniences and material prosperity of the West—in other words, to show them what they are missing in life. This only raises anger at the West—in part, out of jealousy, and in part, at the "heresy" of departing from the simple and impoverished purity of seventh century Islam. The message to these new converts is never a direct denunciation of luxuries or technology. Rather, it is this: "We know you live in a police state and we know you live in poverty. The reason for it all is this: Satan is doing this to you. Satan is the West. Come join our holy war to fight the West."

Islamic nations have tended to have highly autocratic regimes in which the rich grow richer and the poor grow poorer. Economic mismanagement has been widespread. A comment made by an Algerian interviewed in a French news magazine is fairly typical of an opinion that seems to be held by many:

> Algeria was once the granary of Rome, and now it has to import cereals to make bread. It is a land of flocks and gardens, and it imports meat and fruit. It is rich in oil and gas, and it has a foreign debt of twenty-five billion dollars and two million unemployed. (Bernard Lewis, *The Middle East—A Brief History of the Last 2,000 Years* [New York: Simon and Schuster, 1995], 385).

A Policy of Appeasement. If moderate Muslims, as opposed to radical Muslims, gain control of an area, the approach taken is still a move toward denigration of Christians and an elimination of many personal freedoms. Another layer of "persecution" is often imposed—a layer I call the "bureaucratic layer."

In order to maintain power in the face of strident and fiery rhetoric from the hard-line zealots, moderate leaders very often take the approach of "appeasement" of the radical Islamic factions. The current call for Arab nations to draw a hard line against terrorists has not been fully heeded, and likely won't be. Appeasement is still the approach of most Middle East governments.

Let me give you an example of how appeasement operates when moderate Muslim leaders attempt to placate radical factions.

Years ago, a church was seized by radical Muslims in the town of Basatten, near Cairo. The Muslims converted the building into a mosque. When Christians complained to the authorities that their property had been taken, police demolished the building, citing that the Christians had not acquired the proper construction permits. Rather than confront the actions of the Muslim militants, the government adopted a hide-behind-the-law approach. This happens again and again.

Egyptian law states that no church may be built or have any alterations, repairs, or improvements without a *presidential decree*. This law was enacted in 1856 following the outline of the "Covenant of Umar." (The statute was placed on the books by the Ottoman Empire when Egypt was one of its colonies.)

In 1972, President Anwar Sadat promised Coptic Christian leaders that he would grant fifty permits a year for church building. However, from 1973 to 1979, he granted a *total* of fifty permits (rather than the three hundred promised). In 1978 and 1979, he gave five permits.

By 1990, hundreds of applications for permits were outstanding. They had accumulated dust in government bureaucratic offices for decades. Some Christian churches had waited as long as twenty-seven years for a permit to build a building, even though the government builds mosques almost daily and pays mosque leaders. President Mubarak reactivated and tightened the 1856 law, making it virtually impossible for new churches to be built or old churches renovated.

Since 1973, to appease radical Muslims, Egypt has passed a number of laws that pave the way for the Koran to be the major source of law in Egypt. Court decisions have set precedents that push non-Muslims more and more into the role of *dhimmi*.

What happens when Christians speak out?

Well, Christians in Egypt did speak out in 1980. Pope Shenouda of the Coptic Church canceled all official Easter festivities in 1980 and restricted the celebration to simple prayers. He refused to accept President Sadat's annual Easter greetings. The members of the Holy Synod (governing body of the Coptic church) retired to the desert monastery of St. Bishay.

Angered at the worldwide press attention caused by these actions, President Sadat attacked Coptic leaders in a speech delivered on May 14 of that year. He accused them of plotting to overthrow his government, of slandering both him and Egypt, and of attempting to foster social discontent. He then placed the

Christian leaders under house arrest and ousted leaders of the synod from their positions of authority within the church. In their place, he appointed a council of bishops, which was to be more responsive to governmental policies.

After Sadat was assassinated in 1981, virtually all of Sadat's political prisoners were released *except* for these Coptic leaders held under house arrest. It was several years before President Mubarak released them and allowed them to resume their duties as ruling elders of the church in Egypt.

Is what happened in Egypt an extreme case? Hardly. It is typical of what has happened in a number of so-called "moderate" Muslim states. Typically, only Muslims are regarded as full citizens with all the rights of citizenship. In Saudi Arabia, which many in the West seem to think is a moderate Arab state, non-Muslims cannot be citizens at all! Also in Saudi Arabia, no Christian church of any kind can be built—not even a room set aside for Christian worship or discussion of Christian principles, even though the Koran admonishes all Muslims to read the Gospels.

One of the statements that Queen Rania of Jordan made on the Oprah Winfrey program was this: "The important thing is the spirit of Islam. That is all about tolerance, about doing good, diversity, equality, and human dignity. The fact that Islam is very tolerant means that it doesn't impose anything on other people."

She could not be more deceived. The "spirit" of Islam is anything but tolerant, even with moderate Muslims in power. It has never been, is not now, and we cannot expect to become tolerant without force to insist that it be tolerant.

We must never lose sight of the fact that Islam has *no* tolerance for freedom of religion or separation of church and state.

Chapter Ten

OUR RESPONSE AS AMERICANS AND AS CHRISTIANS

What can and should we as Americans and Christians do in fighting against terror? Our political leaders have set forth a policy—but what can we do as individuals?

Below, I offer twelve suggestions. I have broken them down into seven political-secular suggestions, actions that all Americans can take regardless of their faith, and five Christian suggestions, which are actions that are spiritual and evangelistic in nature.

Our Response As Americans

I heartily recommend the following seven actions:

1. Continued Use of Force in Combating Terrorism. Before September 11, terrorism was met with "negotiation."

After September 11, terrorism has been met with a move toward its destruction. The difference is dramatic.

We should be encouraged that American confrontation of Islamic extremism in Afghanistan did not impact Afghanistan alone. Kuwait, just a few months ago, was the on the verge of aligning its criminal code with Islamic law—adopting many of the practices that were instituted under the Taliban in

Afghanistan. After the United States and other Western military forces, in association with the Northern Alliance troops in Afghanistan, brought about the downfall of the Taliban, the fervor for Islamic law in Kuwait was quickly dampened. Kuwaiti officials, who saw the scenes of Afghans rejoicing at the abolition of religious restrictions, seemed ready to abandon their call for stricter enforcement of Islamic law.

We need to support our men and women in the military and let our elected officials know that we will *not* tire of the national effort to root out terrorist cells in operation around the world. We must join our political leaders in adopting a "long-haul" stance when it comes to military action against terrorism.

2. Press for Marginalization of Radical Muslims. The United States needs to continue to press nations to marginalize radical Islamists within their borders.

We need to openly applaud and publicly support those Muslims who call for Muslims to exhibit a greater tolerance for religions other than their own. Just recently these statements have been made:

- An Arab journalist, Ahmad al-Sarraf, recently said on an Al Jazeera TV program, "Why don't we have tolerance? This rhetoric of hatred is in all sermons, in all schoolbooks . . . . We don't need America to interfere and teach us how to worship, but we need a certain element to force us to change our curriculum that calls for extremism." (Thomas L. Friedman, "Spiritual Missile Shield," *www.nytimes.com*, December 6, 2001).

- A liberal Kuwaiti political scientist, Shafeeq Ghabra, said in a debate on Al Jazeera TV: "The Lebanese civil war was not an American creation; neither was the Iran-Iraq war; neither was bin Laden. These are our creations. We need to look inside. We cannot be in this blame-others mode forever." (Thomas L. Friedman, "Fighting bin Ladenism," *www.nytimes.com*, November 6, 2001).

Those who voice such sentiments need to be acknowledged and lifted up as good examples to other Muslims.

We need to get out a strong message that the United States is *not* responsible in any way for what happened on September 11. Islamic extremists are responsible. Those who harbor terrorists are responsible. *And* those who encourage terrorist rhetoric and support prejudice and anger against the United States are responsible.

Veteran Middle East and military analyst Ze'ev Schiff has written,

> There are those who claim that, because Arabs and Muslims feel that they are discriminated against, they are led to carry out acts of terrorism. However, they are not the only ones in the world who sense that they are victims of prejudice. No one has heard any reports of Hindus or Buddhists who are discriminated against (and many of them are victims of prejudice), putting in motion an operation to blow up skyscrapers and major government facilities in the U.S.
>
> It is the responsibility of the Muslims themselves, especially Muslim religious leaders, to prove that these grave acts of terrorism are contrary to the tenets of Islam. The Muslims will not be able to justify such acts by attributing them to the Israeli-Palestinian dispute, which is what they tried to do at the conference of Islamic States in Qatar. Five of the twelve resolutions passed at that gathering concerned Israel and the terrorism it allegedly carries out. In one of the remaining seven resolutions, the delegates did not forget to propose donations to the Afghan people—that is, to the Taliban government. (*Ha'aretz*, October 22, 2001)

We need to call the Islamic States into accountability for their policy of appeasement and support for radical factions.

Here at home, we need to speak out openly against those who advocate loyalty to Islam before loyalty to our fellow citizens.

Across the United States, sixty-nine percent of Arab Muslims have been in favor of "all-out war against countries which harbor or aid terrorists." (Results of a Zogby International poll conducted in October 2001). That may sound like a good number—certainly it is a majority—but what that poll also reveals is that thirty-one percent of Arab Muslims are *not* in favor of moving against nations that harbor or aid terrorists. Why not? Do they see terrorism as valuable or laudable? Do they believe Osama bin Laden is a noble person? Are they among the fringe that have openly labeled the "real terrorists" as the "illegitimate Zionist regime"—in other words, Jews and Israel?

We need to confront these opinions in public forums—live events in which Muslims present their "moderate" opinions, on the editorial pages of our nation's newspapers, and on call-in radio programs.

I certainly am not advocating fomenting hate against Muslims or against Arabs. I am advocating open debate on ideas that apparently are held by thirty-one percent of Muslim Americans. Let's get those ideas out into the open where they can be discussed, argued, and debated. Let's not tolerate terrorist thinking in our own midst without direct, well-reasoned confrontation.

3. Preemptive Strikes When Necessary. The United States has not been known for preemptive strikes. Now such strikes may be necessary.

Preemptive strikes, of course, certainly are preferable to retaliatory strikes—the former prevents tragedy and chaos in the United States, the later responds to tragedy and chaos. The day is likely to come in the near future when the United States finds itself facing a decision: strike now or retaliate later, and not just against a small terrorist cell in Afghanistan, Yemen, Somalia, or Indonesia, but against a major sponsor of terrorism such as Iran or Iraq.

Iran's Hashemi Rafsanjani spoke not long ago of the glorious day "when the Islamic world acquires atomic weapons." He acknowledged that Islamic nations would likely suffer damage in a nuclear exchange, but only one great nuclear blast "would destroy Israel completely." (William Safire, "Arafat's Implausible Denials," *www.nytimes.com,* January 10, 2002)

Three largely Islamic nations have nuclear weapons. One is Pakistan, who likely would not be as concerned about Israel as about its neighbor, India. One is Iran, where scientists already have the know-how and are only in need of raw materials and opportunity. And one is Iraq, whose nuclear development is aided by Russia despite American protests.

Both Iran and Iraq have populations that long for political and religious freedom, and both populations would regard the destruction of Israel as a major coup for their nations. Of the two nations, Israeli leaders Yitzhak Rabin and Ariel Sharon are on record stating that they believe radical Iran poses a much greater danger to Israel. Experts in the United States consider Saddam Hussein of greater immediate threat.

4. An Alternative to OPEC Oil. We in the United States must find an alternative to OPEC oil. The United States is the world's largest oil importer. By the way, the Soviet Union was the world's largest oil producer and it was virtually energy self-sufficient. Many of the former Soviet provinces, now nations, are major oil producers. Some of these are predominantly Muslim in population, others are not.

Surely as a nation we are creative and innovative and technologically skilled enough to come up with viable alternatives that can be implemented in a widespread fashion.

I frequently encounter people who believe America need not strive for energy independence. They believe the cost would be too high, the social disruption too great. They take the approach—let Americans produce wheat and computers, let the Arabs provide oil, and we will all maintain the status quo.

My response is this: You are assuming that economics is a matter of mathematics. To believe this is to totally discount the religious dimension. Muslim states have many people—not just "terrorists"—who believe that the West should be dominated, or eliminated from power, through humiliation. Those who are extremists are willing to die in opposing the infidel to win instant paradise.

Until we gain energy self-sufficiency in the United States, we will not be free of the *political* influence that OPEC nations can exert on us.

Osama bin Laden as a Muslim "leader," and Al Qaeda as an organization, did not simply want to destroy the two tallest skyscrapers and at least one, if not more, buildings that are political icons in the United States. Their purpose was not merely to give the United States a humiliating black eye. The World Trade Center towers—indeed, the entire complex, much of which was heavily damaged or destroyed collaterally to the two towers—were at the *financial* heart of New York City, the United States, and in many ways, the Western world. These terrorists were taking aim at our economy, as well as our world influence economically—as much as they were taking aim at our political strength and political ideology. It has been noted that virtually no Arab financial interests were housed in the World Trade Center towers—the upper floors of those towers had firms that were operated to a great extent by people with Jewish and Christian ideological roots.

Subsequent economic damage was incurred in the fall of the stock markets of the West, and especially the United States. With the tumbling stock markets came massive lay-offs and a lack of income to major industries in the United States, especially the airline industry, tourism as a whole, and virtually all sectors of the retail market.

Oil profits funded the attacks of September 11—if not directly, indirectly. Oil profits funded terrorism in the past. It will continue to fund terrorism.

5. Tighter Foreign Investment Laws. We must tighten our foreign investment laws in the United States. American commercial centers would be in chaos such as we have never seen if OPEC investors suddenly liquidated their assets, dumped their United States Treasury bills on the market, or transferred their liquid assets away from the United States. I will not presume to give specifics as to how our investment laws should be modified—I'll leave that to the experts. But what I do believe we need to do as individual citizens is to ask our elected representatives to protect our economy from manipulation by foreign investors by instituting *strong* safeguards.

Those who do business with Muslim governments or Muslim individuals need to make certain that no religious strings are attached to their business dealings. Certainly there are no foolproof ways to determine this—nobody can dictate how a farmland or a bank, for example, might be used after such properties are sold. We should, however, become "wise as serpents" in our use of resources.

It wasn't that long ago that *Al Ahram* (the official newspaper of Egypt) called for Arabs to use their economic muscle—at the time, $200 billion invested in the United States—to get what they wanted.

Should the "coalition" against terrorist cell groups fall apart, which I predict is inevitable given the great disparity of ideology between the West and the Arab world, we must be prepared for

OPEC nations to classify us openly as enemies. If that happens, the disturbance in our society is likely to be enormous.

6. Press for Full Human Rights in Islamic Nations. We need to encourage our elected officials to continue to press for full human rights for the citizens of Islamic nations. Christians, as well as Jews and those of any other religion, should be allowed to practice the religion of their choice in any nation of the world. This is a fundamental human right.

Many Americans do not seem to be aware that literally hundreds of millions of dollars in "aid" is given by the United States and Europe to several Muslim nations. This does not include the vast amount of non-profit aid given to impoverished Muslims, largely in the form of goods and services (including Western volunteer workers).

We should openly ask oil-rich Muslims and Muslims in America why they aren't using their wealth to support their "weaker" and poorer Muslim brothers.

If we are to be benefactors to the world, surely we can tie our benevolent charity to the causes that we consider to be inalienable rights (as stated by the Declaration of Independence and the Bill of Rights of the United States Constitution).

The United States federal government requires that colleges and universities in the United States be free of racial, ethnic, and religious prejudice before federal money will be granted in the form of either financial aid or institutional grants, including research grants. This rule is in effect for both private and public institutions. Why shouldn't the United States require foreign nations to extend the same freedom of racial, ethnic, or religious prejudices prior to the granting of federal money in the form of foreign aid, investment, or military assistance? After all, federal money is money generated (earned) by American citizens, American companies, and companies operating on American soil using American labor and resources. We as private citizens should voice our concern about how our tax dollars are used on the international stage, and do so with a loud, focused political voice.

The nations of the Christian West, and particularly the United States, have long declared themselves to be protectors of the oppressed. Perhaps we should be using that influence to help

Christians, Jews, and other minorities in the nations of the Middle East, including Israel.

Our policies regarding human rights should be clear, firm, and coherent. We should construct our foreign policy on the firm basis of justice, rather than on the basis of immediate economic gain or political interests.

Very directly, we should press for freedom of speech and freedom of religion in nations that receive our aid—as well as press for these freedoms in nations that do not. Non-Muslims should be allowed freedom to engage in their religious practices. They should be allowed to build schools, educational centers, and places of worship without government imposed limitations. They should be allowed to advertise their activities and to distribute materials related to their faith. We afford these freedoms to Muslims in America. Muslim nations should afford those freedoms to Christians in their lands.

I also contend that Christian missionaries should be allowed to speak openly about the *Injeil* (Gospels) in Muslim lands.

7. Defense Against Terrorism. I strongly support our government's Homeland Defense efforts. We must do our best to protect ourselves in every way possible, and no longer "live and let live" if we see others in our neighborhoods acting in a way that appears suspicious or potentially evil. In addition, we must not allow anti-democratic Islamic laws to be incorporated into their bodies of law (which are based largely on Judeo-Christian values). We must maintain a defensive posture against any group or organization that seeks to diminish the basic freedoms of the Bill of Rights.

These are basic actions that I heartily advocate *all* freedom-loving Americans should take. Beyond these actions are ones that I believe *Christians* should take.

Our Response As Christians

As Christians we must:

1. Become Fully Informed. A United States Congressman —a man who serves on high-ranking committees, is well-traveled, and well-versed on the current wave of terrorism—referred to terrorists on a national news program in January 2002 as people who have "mischief in their hearts" and "bad thoughts." From my perspective, the situation is far beyond that. If that is the prevailing mindset of Americans, we are sadly in need of a *great* deal more information.

We must seek to understand as much as we can about the character and objectives of modern Islamic fundamentalism. We must become familiar with the teachings of Islam and the tenets of the Muslim religion. We must open our eyes to the serious threat Islam poses to the Western cultures. We must be aware that Muslims in the West will only tell us what they know we want to hear. The challenge is for us personally to examine the tenets of Islam.

Those who are informed must speak up. Government officials, church people, corporate leaders, and the mass media all need to be alerted to the truth.

2. Develop a Christian Apologetic. Christians must be prepared to explain their basic Christian beliefs. Many Christians need to revisit, for example, their own understanding of the Trinity. One of the most popular tracts handed out by Muslim students on American college and university campuses is a tract that claims Christians believe in three gods rather than one. Many Christians don't have a response—they don't understand one of their core beliefs, the doctrine of the Trinity. That doctrine, simply stated, is that there is only one true God, and yet within the being of God from all eternity there has always existed a bond of relationship, love, and intimacy: Father, and Son, and Holy Spirit.

At least one seminary is moving in this direction. Southern Evangelical Seminary in Charlotte, N.C., has announced the establishment of an "Institute of Islamic Studies" to begin the summer of 2002. The first course will be "Islamic Apologetics," with an emphasis placed on answering Islam's charges against Christianity. ("Doug Potter, "Southern Evangelical Seminary Dives into Islam" *Charlotte World* [January 2002])

We as individual Christians need to develop an apologetic to counter the false claims of Islam. Ask yourself, "What would I say if a Muslim told me what he believes to be true about Christianity? How would I respond to a Muslim's take on his own religion?"

3. Pray. As Christians we must pray and intercede for Muslims. That is our first and foremost responsibility. We must pray that God will sovereignly and supernaturally open the door for the

Gospel in Muslim nations, and that God's power will be manifested strongly to convict people of their need of the Savior, Jesus Christ. We must pray against the spirits of fear, self-justification, hatred, revenge, death, bloodshed, lying, and lust—at the same time, praying and believing that those who are held captive by spiritual forces will be freed by the power of faith in Christ Jesus.

We must pray:

- that God will protect the cause of liberty and freedom and intervene directly in mercy for those who are being oppressed and persecuted for the sake of the Gospel.

- for protection and provision for all of our fellow Christians, and especially for those who are new to the Christian faith that they will stand firm in their faith.

- that God will intervene, using whatever supernatural (or natural) forces He chooses to employ, to bring terrorists to justice and expose future terrorist plots.

Praying against the Spirit of Fear. We especially need to pray against the spirit of fear that keeps many Muslims from leaving Islam. Islam teaches its adherents that to turn from Islam is to become an infidel who will be plagued by the devil and demons (*jinn*), and experience with certainty the wrath of Allah and hell after death.

Time and again, Muslims who have accepted Christ tell that at their first hearing of the Gospel, they felt great fear. They fear God, fear resisting Muhammad, fear Islam, fear they may have believed in error in the past, and fear they will go to hell in the future. Generally speaking, the more they know about Jesus, the greater the fear they feel.

This fear is not unfounded. Historically speaking, those who convert to Christianity (or any other religion) pay a very high price, especially those who are raised in strict Muslim homes. Apostasy in Islam means rejection of Islam by action or word of mouth. Punishment for apostasy is death.

Even if they are not killed, those who leave Islam stand to lose everything they own and every relationship with everyone they love. At worst, they lose their lives. Even those who do accept Jesus as their Savior often have intense bouts of deep fear.

Fear is the stronghold of any false religion. It must be confronted first and foremost in the spiritual realm—and that means intense and prolonged prayer.

4. Increase Christian Evangelistic Efforts. We must double our efforts to reach the world with the gospel of Jesus Christ.

Former Muslims, now Christians, tell me repeatedly that they had a longstanding hunger in their hearts for the truth of God, but they did not know Jesus because they had never heard of Him. While they may have heard His "name" or heard the word "Christianity," they did not truly know what Jesus said, did, or the purpose for His life as revealed in the New Testament.

Here are basic requirements for this evangelistic effort on a *personal* level:

- Ask God to give you a heart for Muslim people—a compassion for them, a willingness to pray for them, and the courage to speak to Muslims God may bring across your path.

- Arm yourself with Scripture. Memorize passages of the Bible that speak to the love and saving grace of Jesus Christ, the love and mercy of God, and the assurance of Christ's forgiveness of sin and gift of eternal life.

- Pray for boldness in your witness to Muslims.

- Ask the Holy Spirit before and while speaking to a Muslim what you should say, and what you should leave unsaid in silence.

- do not berate a Muslim for his or her beliefs. But do speak the truth in as loving, calm, and spiritually assured tone of voice as possible.

- Speak boldly what you know to be true about Jesus and do not compromise or argue. Simply state what you know to be truth. Refuse to in any way compromise what you believe about Jesus—for example, do not say, "Well, what you believe is what you believe, and what I believe is what I believe." Stand strong for what you know to be the truth about Jesus and salvation: "Salvation is found in no one else, for there is no other name under heaven given to men by which we must be saved." (Acts 4:12)

- if the person will allow you to pray, then pray in the powerful name of Jesus. (Acts 4:12) Muslims believe that Jesus can heal, perform miracles, and even raise the dead.

- Trust the Holy Spirit to work in the person's life. The Holy Spirit is the One who convicts. He is the One who opens the eyes of the blind. He is the One who leads a person to accept Jesus. He is the One who delivers from evil.

Here is what we can do as *churches and Christian organizations:*

- The Gospel speaks for itself. Even as we give copies of the Gospels to Muslims, we must pray that Muslims *will read* what has been made available to them. We should pray that Muslims will discover the divine riches of the Gospel's truth. Surely Christ was speaking to all people when He said, "You will know the truth, and the truth will set you free." (John 8:32)

- Make a concerted outreach to Muslim women. More than five hundred million Muslims are women—the three foremost characteristics of a Muslim woman are: she is illiterate, she is poor, and she lives in a village. Jesus held women in high regard and gave them equal access to the gospel. Muslim women need to know that.

5. Reach Out to Muslims in Love. One of the greatest antidotes for fear is this: "the truth conveyed in love." We must love Muslims the way Jesus loves them. The Bible says, "Perfect love drives out fear." (1 John 4:18)

Many Muslims are feeling threatened and rejected in the United States. This is an ideal time for Christians to reach out to their immediate neighbors and to build a bridge of friendship. Invite Muslims to your home for a meal (no alcohol or pork). Don't be afraid to pray in their presence. You may want to invite them to a Christian Bible study, couching the invitation in terms of a means of furthering "mutual understanding." Give a Muslim neighbor a New Testament in his or her native language (if it isn't English).

Very often, the Muslim must first accept the love of God before he can hear fully the salvation that Jesus Christ makes possible.

Speak openly and with tenderness to Muslims about God's great love.

Not only do people reflect in their behavior toward others their belief toward God, but also people become what they *fear*. Muslims have great internal fear about Allah's judgment and condemnation. They, in turn, become judgmental and condemning. According to Islam, grace and forgiveness are rare attributes of God, and they are even more rare in the lives of Muslims. A common saying in the Islamic world declares, "Islam is as arid as the deserts of its birth."

Newly converted Muslims need to be told with authority and great love that they need not be afraid of Allah any longer, that God loves them, and that He is not angry with them. Just as fear binds the hearts of Muslims, so love brings them release from fear. Once a Muslim has a real taste of God's divine love, fear vanishes.

We must couple our expressions of love with moral goodness. Muslims cannot accept the truth of the Gospel if we do not live loving and morally exemplary lives.

We must live individually and collectively as strong Christians. We must learn the principle of loving those with whom we disagree, without being weak or passive. Firmness and compassion are not mutually exclusive. We must speak and act with spiritual authority, yet without arrogance. In many ways, we need to *learn* how to do this, especially when dealing with people of other cultures.

We must display true moral strength to Muslims. We must be living examples of godliness and "love in action" within our own families and in our associations with all other people, and especially those we call Christian brothers and sisters.

A Plan for Action

I hope you will take these twelve areas of action to heart. Write letters. Make calls. Enroll in courses. Think. Discuss. And above all, make a plan of action for *personally* reaching out to Muslims with the GOOD NEWS of God's love and saving power.

I close as I began, with this statement: I love the Muslim people. I do not look down on them. To the contrary, I yearn for them to know the fullness of life that comes only through Jesus Christ.